# On Wheel and On Foot

## 61 walks for the able and disabled in Lancashire and Cumbria

Compiled by

The Rotary Clubs of Lancashire and Cumbria

and edited by

Fred Harrison

*This book is dedicated to the memory of*
*Ron Johnston*

*We wish to thank Ron's wife Betty*
*and his sons Ian and Michael*
*for their interest and support for this venture*

---

*On Wheel and on Foot*

compiled by The Rotary Clubs of Lancashire and Cumbria (District 1190), and edited by Fred Harrison

Copyright,© The Rotary Clubs of Lancashire and Cumbria

Published by The Rotary Clubs of Lancashire and Cumbria (District 1190)
Typeset in 10½/12 Caslon by Carnegie Publishing Ltd., Preston
Printed by T. Snape & Co. Ltd., Boltons Court, Preston

**ISBN 0 948789 78 6**

# Acknowledgements

Mr. J. D. Dolan, Lancashire County Librarian
Mr. Philip G. Luff, Recreation and Conservation Officer, North West Water
for their interest and advice.
Alder Grange High School, Rawtenstall.
Mrs. Angela Nuttall and Mrs. Deborah Garner, for secretarial help.
Past District Governor Glyn Morgan.
Rotarian Robert M. Driver, Des.RCA, for the cover illustration.
Rotarian Ray Pollard, whose efforts made this book possible.
Rotarian Fred Harrison, editor.
Members of the Rotary Club of Rossendale
and all Rotarians in District 1190
who have contributed to this publication.

# Sponsors

Members of the Rotary Club of Rossendale wish to thank the following sponsors for their generous support of this project:

The National Westminster Bank
British Nuclear Fuels
Cumbria County Council
J. B. Broadley
E. Sutton & Sons
North West Water Authority
Lancashire County Council
Rossendale Borough Council
T.N.T.
British Gas
Hurstwood Developments
Lambert Howorth plc
Rossendale Lions
Bacup Shoe Company
Lancashire Constabulary

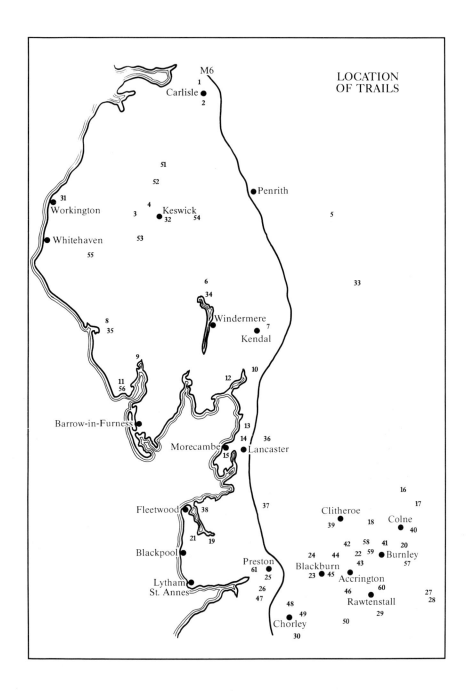

LOCATION
OF TRAILS

M6
1
Carlisle ●
2

51

52

● Penrith

● 31
Workington
3 4 Keswick
● 32 54

5

53
● Whitehaven
55

33

6
34

● Windermere
7
Kendal

8
35

9

10

11
56
12

Barrow-in-Furness ●

13

14 36
Morecambe ● ● Lancaster
15

16

17

Fleetwood ● 38
37
Clitheroe
●
39 18 Colne
●
40

21
19

42 58 41 20
Blackpool ●
24 44 22 59 ● Burnley
23 43 57
Preston 61 Blackburn
● 45 Accrington
25 60
Lytham
St. Annes
26 46 27
47 Rawtenstall 28
48
49 29
Chorley 50
30

iv

# Contents

# How the idea began

The idea for a publication outlining suitable trails for wheelchair-bound people originated when a much respected member of the Rossendale Rotary Club, Ron Johnston, was struck by the severely disabling motor neurone disease. From a healthy ex-policeman with a love of the open air and fell walking, he was reduced to an invalid in a wheelchair, becoming more and more helpless as the illness took its inevitable toll.

Missing those outdoor activities, Ron mooted the idea of trails in which the disabled could take part locally, and this led the club to explore the possibility of extending the idea to cover the whole of Cumbria and Lancashire. Thanks to the co-operation of the members of the Rotary Clubs in this area (Rotary District 1190), here is the result.

Ron, who hailed from Workington, spent his working life in the Lancashire Constabulary, and came to Rossendale as a Chief Inspector, and then as a Superintendent in charge of the local sub-division. He joined the Rossendale Rotary Club in 1969 and served as its president nine years later. In 1989, when he could not attend meetings regularly because of his disability, he was considering resignation with reluctance. The club did not wish to lose such a valued member and, to his great delight, elected him as an honorary member. Sadly, he died in March the following year, but the idea which he had put into operation means that his memory will live on.

# Introduction

We hope that this book will encourage handicapped people and their friends to make more use of our beautiful countryside. The book contains 61 walks divided into three categories. The walks have been provided by members of the Rotary Clubs in District 1190 (Lancashire and Cumbria). This accounts for the individuality of the walks. The Rotary Club of Rossendale is very grateful to the members of these Rotary Clubs for trying and testing the walks before recommending them.

The 'A' walks are the easiest type. They are on reasonable terrain and are possible for two senior citizens of imperfect health to accomplish. These walks include town trails, parks and promenades. We hope you will find them interesting and enjoyable.

The 'B' walks are more energetic and cover distances of four to eight miles. Most of these walks are circular, but where the walk is linear the distance shown is there *and* back. The walks include country paths, road trails with good views and treks over moorland or round scenic reservoirs.

The 'C' walks are for the more adventurous, younger wheelchair users, with two or three fit helpers. Distances vary from four to twelve miles, but all contain some stretches of hilly and/or rough terrain.

Wherever possible there are details of the nearest toilet facilities for the disabled; also the nearest cafes, inns and/or hotels are listed.

Some of the walks have sketch maps to assist with directions. For the longer or more complex walks, however, it may be advisable to use the relevant Ordnance Survey Pathfinder maps.

We hope you find your walks manageable, interesting and, above all, enjoyable.

# A Day Out at Talkin Tarn

## Starting Point

We can leave Carlisle either by the B5264 north of the river towards Brampton or south of the river on the A69. The former is probably preferable, and a few miles from Carlisle one passes the airfields whose commercial usefulness is always under discussion.

The A69 takes one through more built-up areas, but one can always digress if time is available. Whichever road one chooses, it is about half an hour's comfortable driving until we reach Brampton.

## Details of Trail

A visit in the area would not be complete without a visit to St. Martin's Anglican Church, which is renowned throughout the country for its stained glass, of which the east window is a magnificent example. Arriving in Brampton, one will immediately see the church off to the right, with a car park adjoining. Pamphlets giving the history of the present St. Martin's Church and its predecessors are on the table by the font. Unfortunately for the disabled, there are steps at the west end which have to be surmounted. However, if accompanied by able-bodied colleagues, a wheelchair could be lifted and the disabled enabled to enter.

Having left the church, one can proceed into Brampton and about two hundred yards on the right one can park outside the Capon Tree Restaurant for some light refreshment and afterwards continue through the town keeping to the right at Moot Hall with clock, and proceed on the Castle Carrock road (B6413) for about one mile over the railway crossing. Turn left shortly afterwards at the sign for the Talkin Tarn, O.S. ref. 545590. Half a mile brings one to a side road to the tarn, on the right.

The tarn is owned by Cumbria County Council and, if necessary, contact on the site can be obtained on 96977 3129. The tarn is situated in a country park of about 180 acres of wood and farmland. There are water activities such as rowing boats, and wind-surfing equipment can be hired. Parking is available for cars

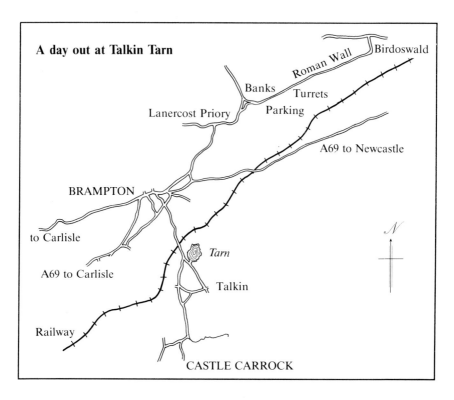

**A day out at Talkin Tarn**

Birdoswald

Roman Wall

Banks

Turrets

Lanercost Priory

Parking

A69 to Newcastle

BRAMPTON

to Carlisle

A69 to Carlisle

Tarn

Talkin

Railway

CASTLE CARROCK

and coaches, and cars can be taken to the edge of the tarn to unload wheelchairs. Toilets are available, but none suitable for the disabled.

There are picnic areas, a shop selling sweets, soft drinks and ice cream, and there is also a vending machine.

The tarn and park are open all year round, Monday to Sunday, and the shop opens 10.00–18.00 hours on Saturday and Sunday between Easter and October, and Monday to Sunday in July and August.

Other places of interest nearby are Lanercost Priory, and Banks Terrace and turrets on the Roman wall.

# Tour of the City of Carlisle

## Starting Point

To reach Carlisle leave the M6 motorway at junction 42 if travelling north, or junction 44 if travelling south. Start the tour outside the Old Town Hall (1). The city centre is pedestrianised, but parking for the disabled is in the centre of the pedestrianised area, i.e. opposite Marks & Spencer, further along English Street towards the traffic lights, and also in Bank Street (disabled badge permits required).

## Details of Trail

The following describes an interesting tour in which to explore the attractions of the city, historical and otherwise. It can be lengthened or shortened depending on one's mobility in a wheelchair.

The Town Hall houses the Tourist Information Centre on the ground floor. Next door, to the left, is the fifteenth-century Guildhall Museum (2) which exhibits relics of the various guilds. Directly opposite the town hall, and recently renovated, is the market cross (3) in the midst of a pedestrian area surrounded by well-known shops.

Cross over the road to Binns and go down St. Cuthbert's Lane leading to the church of that name (4),

which is Carlisle's parish church and was re-built in 1778. Passing through Heads Lane by Marks & Spencer to West Walls (5), one is on a road which traverses the upper part of the city wall.

On the opposite pavement by the wall is an entrance to the Sally Port steps (6), known as such because of the practice of 'sallying forth' in secret when the city was besieged.

Turning right at the end of Heads Lane and continuing, one passes the entrance to the tithe barn (7) which, as its name implies, was used as a collection centre of taxes and tithes for the priory.

Continuing past the entrance to Church House (8) and the Diocesan

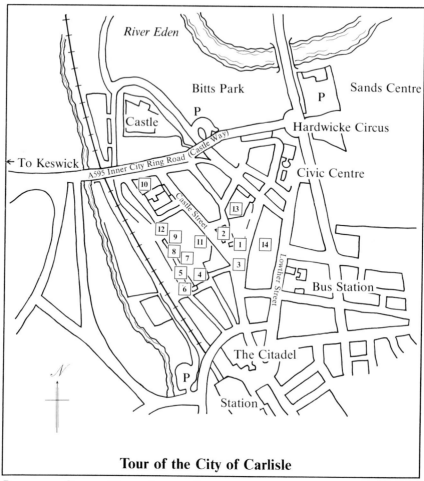

**Tour of the City of Carlisle**

Resources Centre (9), a short walk brings one to Paternoster Row. Turn right, and another short walk leads to the head of Abbey Street on the left. Immediately on the right is the west door entrance to the cathedral grounds. There is now a choice of entering the grounds or walking down Abbey Street for two or three hundred yards, on the right of which are the grounds of Tullie House Museum and Art Gallery (10). An exciting £5m project by the City Council has resulted in a modern multi-purpose museum and art gallery for the city. There is a charge for entrance to the Border Galleries on the first floor, which tell the story of the natural and historical heritage of the region. The complex contains a new contemporary art gallery, shopping complex, cafe, restaurant, and function room, and there is access for the disabled.

Leave Tullie House by the opposite gate, coming out on to Castle Street, turn right and walk towards the corner of the cathedral (11) and the other end of Paternoster Row, then turn right towards the west door and enter. Here are the residences of the clergy and staff. The buttery (12) is on the right, and on the left is the south and main door to the cathedral. A word with the verger or a guide will produce a portable ramp for ease of access. Once inside, there are ramps and assistance available to negotiate difficult steps, and a loop system to enable the hard of hearing to participate in the services. The cathedral can be visited daily between 8.00am and 7.00pm. The buttery is open all year, Mondays to Saturdays between 10.00am and 4.00pm, serving cold meals and hot snacks. Unfortunately there are no ramp facilities for the disabled here, but visitors unable to manage the steps down into the buttery could have food brought outside if the weather is congenial, and there is a picnic area. There are toilets but, again, these do not cater for the physically disabled.

From the cathedral, leave the grounds by the iron gates at the east end into Castle Street, cross the road and proceed down St. Mary's Gate with the Cumberland Building Society on the right. At the bottom is the entrance to the covered market (13), which is open daily and has a wide variety of stalls. Enter and make for the opposite side, which brings one out on Scotch Street, on the opposite side of which is the modern Lanes (14), a shopping centre constructed on the site of original buildings and shops between which were narrow lanes.

Refreshments can be obtained at the coffee shop, near which are toilets for the disabled. Nearby lifts (large enough for wheelchairs) and an escalator provide access to the library on the first floor. Leave the Lanes and return to the old town hall.

Other places of interest which can be reached by car are Sands Leisure Centre (where refreshments are available and toilets for the disabled), and the Castle and Border Regimental Museum, open daily from 9.30am (Sundays 2.00pm).

# Mirehouse Woodland and Lakeside Walk, near Keswick

## Starting Point

Take the A591 from Keswick to Bassenthwaite. At an approximate distance of three miles, at Dodd Wood, on the right hand side of the road is the site of the old sawmill, now converted into tea rooms and car park. This is the start of the trail, and one must purchase a ticket here for access to the walk.

---

## Details of Trail

The Mirehouse grounds and house are open between 1st April and 31st October each year. The grounds are normally open from 10.30am to 5.30pm each day and the house (an English manor with literary connections) is open to the public on Sundays, Wednesdays and Bank Holiday Mondays. Admission to the grounds is £1.80 for adults, 70p for children; and to the manor house 90p for adults, 50p for children (1990 charges).

The walk, about 1½ miles, is marked by posts with yellow bands round the top. A booklet is available which describes the walk and the house. The trail gives access to Bassenthwaite lakeside and to St. Begas Church, believed to be tenth century.

Facilities: The Old Saw Mill, Dodd Wood, Keswick, tel. Keswick 74317. Toilets on car park not really suitable, but Calvert Trust Hostel nearby is open daily until 4.30pm; The Snooty Fox Inn, Uldale, tel: 0965 7479. The inn is accessible to wheelchairs and is about two miles from Castle Inn crossroads, along the A591 towards Bothel/Cockermouth.

# Friar's Crag, Keswick

## *Starting Point*

Leave the M6 at junction 40 (Keswick–Penrith) and take the A66 to Keswick. Ignore the first signpost off the A66 into Keswick, and continue to the roundabout, following the signs to the left at the roundabout into Keswick. At the junction at the bottom of the road, turn left into the town centre, and then right at the sign to Central car park and Lakeside car park. Follow the road round past the Central car park on the left to a mini-roundabout. Turn right here, and the Lakeside car park will be on your left after about one hundred yards. Total length of walk, approximately one mile.

## *Details of Trail*

Leave the car park adjacent to the Century Theatre (which is a blue box on wheels!), and follow the road down to the water's edge and boat landing. The path continues along the edge of the lake, with numerous seating areas where one can pause to watch the boats and ducks on the lake, or look across to Derwent Isle and the hills beyond. The first quarter-mile of the walk is on tarmacadam, turning to a gravel path which is generally level, but can be a bit bumpy towards the end of the walk. It is well worth making the effort to get to the end of the path to see the magnificent view of the length of Derwentwater and the surrounding hills. The very last part of the walk to the best viewing point requires some care.

Facilities: there are toilets for the disabled adjacent to the lakeside car park or central car park. National key system – if no key, you can borrow one from the Information Centre, Moot Hall, in Keswick town centre. King's Arms Hotel, Main Street, Keswick, tel: 71108 – level entrance, toilets not ideal for wheel-chairs, bar and restaurant food. Oddfellow Arms, Main Street, Keswick, tel: 72682 – level entrance, can be busy in season, real ale, good bar food, toilets not ideal for wheel-chairs. Johnson's, Station Street, Keswick – self-service restaurant, mainly snack foods, level entrance, toilets not suitable for wheelchairs.

Trail 5
Grade A

# Eden River Bank and Appleby Town Walk

## *Starting Point*

Approach the market square in the centre of Appleby from the A66 which runs from Brough to Penrith, or from the B6260 from Kendal. Take the one-way street called High Wiend down by the side of the post office to the car park in Chapel Street, following the swimming pool signs only as far as Harrison's garage. Park opposite (there is a small charge).

# Details of Trail

Follow the footpath from the park to the river, and walk upstream along the river bank to the swimming pool, children's playground and round to the cricket field, where seats and shelters are conveniently situated to watch the matches. Otherwise, you can just sit by the river and watch the world go by.

Leave the river bank where the path meets Bridge Street and turn right along the narrow pavement to the market square. Continue toward St. Lawrence's Church cloisters and, if you have time, look round this lovely old church. From the front of the cloisters you will see the Low Cross, the imposing Tufton Arms Hotel, the ancient moot hall (with Tourist Information Office) and, immediately adjacent, the entrance to the public hall with disabled toilet facilities. You can now continue back to the car park by Low Wiend which lies between the cloisters and the Crown & Cushion public house.

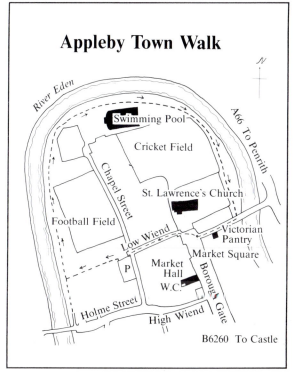

**Appleby Town Walk**

River Eden · Swimming Pool · Cricket Field · A66 To Penrith · St. Lawrence's Church · Chapel Street · Football Field · Low Wiend · Victorian Pantry · Market Square · P · Market Hall · W.C. · Borough Gate · Holme Street · High Wiend · B6260 To Castle

This is a comparatively easy and very pleasant walk, mostly on asphalt paths, but with a long, grass stretch. There are short cuts back to the car park should the weather suddenly change, and there are no obstacles such as narrow gateways or steps.

Time – twenty to forty minutes, or as long as you wish.

Additionally, one could visit Appleby Castle to view the castle itself and its unique collection of

wildfowl and tropical species, but the going is harder. Parking is, however, available in the grounds. The castle is open 10.00am to 5.00pm from Easter to 30th September.

Meals and Refreshments: Victorian Pantry on Bridge Street near the market square offers access for wheelchairs and is open for good coffee, teas and luncheons from 10.00am to 5.30pm daily (11.00am to 5.30pm Sundays, and mornings only on Thursdays during the winter).

In the castle grounds there is a cafe offering similar fare, but wheelchair access is more difficult. There are picnic tables just inside the entrance to the castle grounds.

Toilets as mentioned in text.

*Trail 6*
*Grade A*

# Grasmere

### Starting Point

Leave the main Ambleside–Keswick (A591) road at the Swan Hotel and drive into Grasmere village. After six hundred yards, turn left and park in the car park behind the village hall (Broadgate car park, GR337076). There are two disabled spaces on the far side opposite the entrance, and parking is free to orange badge holders.

# Details of Trail

Grasmere is in the heart of the Lake District and consequently gets very busy during the peak holiday season. This trail makes a lovely walk in the early evening (when all the trippers are scurrying back home), or at any time out of season.

Cross the footbridge leading from the car park and follow the riverside path. The views of the fells are spectacular. Looking towards the mountain pass of Dunmail Raise, once the ancient border between England and Scotland, on your left is Helm Crag with lion and lamb rock-shapes on the summit, and on your right are the sweeping fells of Seat Sandal and Stone Arthur.

The riverside path leads into the heart of the village, finishing next to St. Oswald's Church. Turn left past Sarah Nelson's Celebrated Ginger-bread Shop and pass through the lychgate and into the churchyard. Turn left immediately, and follow the sign for Wordsworth's grave. Here lie William and Dorothy Wordsworth, plus numerous others of their family.

Leave the churchyard by the other gate and cross over the road – a bit tricky – and to the right enter the grounds of Grasmere Garden Centre. You may wish to browse here or continue skirting the right hand side of the building, passing the Tourist Information Office. Regain the road.

Turning left, the next portion follows Red Bank Road past the Gold Rill Hotel, round a bend, and comes to a small cafe situated on the shore of Grasmere Lake. Here you can enjoy a snack on the lakeside lawn, and even hire a rowing boat. Note that access to the cafe is down two smallish steps.

After gazing over the beauty of Grasmere, return to the village the same way. At the Tourist Information Office turn left, passing Tweedie's Bar and the Rowan Tree wholefood restaurant, and back into the centre of the village.

Continue past the gallery of the famous Lakeland painter, Heaton Cooper (one step entrance). Opposite is Moss Parrock, a small grassy area off which there is a disabled persons' toilet locked with the radar key.

Gain the pavement across the road from Sam Read's bookshop and wander along the public park. Cross the road, enter the park and follow the perimeter path to the car park.

# A walk round Kirkland (the original Kendal) and a riverside stroll

## Starting Point

Approaching Kendal from the south, i.e. from the A591 (A6) from the M6 and Lancaster, follow the one-way system into Kendal. After traffic merges from the right across Nether Bridge, take the right hand lane and turn into the Parish Church car park on the right, opposite Carlson's fishing tackle shop. The car park is pay and display.

## Details of Trail

Turn right out of the car park into Kirkland, passing the Ring o' Bells pub on your left. You are now standing in the oldest part of Kendal, known as Kirkland (the church land), which existed as a separate township right up until 1908 when it became part of the Borough of Kendal.

Look across the road to the buildings opposite. Between Cobbler John and the Wheatsheaf you can see a narrow alley called Kirkbarrow Lane, which is Kendal's smallest, narrowest yard, and is known locally as 'T'Crack'.

Go through the decorated iron gates into the churchyard and pause just outside the Parish Church of the Holy and Undivided Trinity. Kendal Parish Church dates from the thirteenth century, and there is some stonework incorporated into the present building from an earlier Saxon church, which may have come from the Roman fort at Water Crook, just south of Kendal. If you have time, do go into the church. The entrance is to the right and is level. Guide books are available inside, and the church is open until 4.30pm daily. Things to see inside the church include:

1.  The Parr Chapel

2. The Bellingham Chapel
3. The Strickland Chapel
4. The helmet and sword of Robin the Devil.

Turn left in front of the church, heading towards the trees, and this will bring you into the Abbot Hall car park. To your right is the Georgian building of Abbot Hall, now an art gallery, and to your left, in the old stable blocks of Abbot Hall, is the Museum of Lakeland Life and Industry. If you have time, both floors of the art gallery are accessible to wheelchair users with assistance. There is a lift, and a couple of stairs to be negotiated, but staff will be happy to assist if they know beforehand (tel. 0539 722464). The gallery is open 10.30am to 5.30pm Monday to Friday, 2.00pm to 5.00pm Saturday and Sunday (Saturdays 10.30am to 5.00pm from Spring Bank Holiday to 31st October). Closed 25th, 26th December and 1st January.

The collection in Abbot Hall was built up from local items and includes work by local portrait painters Daniel Gardner and George Romney, together with landscape paintings from the eighteenth century. Upstairs there are exhibitions of contemporary art, and Abbot Hall hosts a temporary exhibition programme throughout the year.

The Museum of Lakeland Life and Industry brings Lakeland's social and economic history to life, and the lower floor is accessible to

wheelchair users. This includes a fascinating display of farm implements in the farm barn. Opening hours and telephone number are the same as for Abbot Hall (see details above).

Go around to the left of Abbot Hall and head towards the River Kent, passing the bowling green on the left. There are seats here if needed. Turn left over the small level footbridge over Blind Beck (now dry except after periods of heavy rain) which marks the old boundary between Kirkland and Kendal, the name 'Blind' deriving from the word 'blaen', meaning 'town end'.

Once over the footbridge, turn right to the River Kent and then left following a path which runs alongside the river. There are picnic tables to the left here, the tables being a suitable height for wheelchair users. When you are alongside the flats on the left, look to your right across the river and over the top of the buildings, and the ruins of Kendal Castle can be seen on Castle Hill, surrounded by a few trees. The exact origins of Kendal Castle are uncertain, but it is likely that it was built as a fortified manor house in the mid-thirteenth century.

Keep to the riverside path until you reach some buildings called Gawith Place on your left. These buildings are named after Samuel Gawith who lived in Highgate, Kendal's main street, in the nineteenth century and the end cottage is a good example of a traditional Kendal domestic dwelling.

Go a little further along and look for the slate panel on the wall to your left, indicating past flood levels. The bridge ahead of you and to the right is known as Miller's Bridge and replaced an earlier wooden one which was washed away in a flood in 1635.

Retrace your footsteps along the riverside path towards Abbot Hall, and the car park is beyond the Parish Church.

Facilities: There are toilets for the disabled in Abbot Hall car park. Turn right past the Museum of Lakeland Life and Industry and go beyond Abbot Hall Craft Shop on the left. The toilets are to the far right-hand side of the car park. (There is a small speed ramp at the entrance to the car park.)

For further information on places to stay, things to see and do in and around Kendal, call in at Kendal Tourist Information Centre, Town Hall, Highgate, Kendal, tel: (0539) 725758.

# Muncaster Castle and grounds

## Starting Point

Leave the M6 at junction 36 and follow the signposts to Barrow. Take the A590 to Greennodd and then the A595 to Muncaster Castle, which is one mile east of Ravenglass.

## Details of Trail

Muncaster Castle has been the home of the Pennington family since the thirteenth century. The pele tower, dating from the time when there was a tower or fort on the site, stands on Roman foundations. The castle is very much 'lived in' and contains superb antique furniture, portraits by famous artists, beautiful tapestries and other articles of historic and artistic merit.

The gardens have a world-wide reputation, being famed for their outstanding collection of rhododendrons and azaleas, which are at their best in May and early June. The gardens contain a wide-ranging display of rare and beautiful trees and exotic shrubs, and the variety of quality plants offered for sale in the garden centre is particularly attractive to visitors.

Muncaster Castle is the headquarters of the British Owl Breeding and Release Scheme (BOBARS), an organisation formed to study owls both in the wild and in captivity, and run by the well-known TV ornithologist Tony Warburton. The aviary houses a comprehensive collection of owls including all of the British species and some from overseas.

Opening times: The castle and grounds are open daily except Mondays (Bank Holidays excepted) from Good Friday to 30th September. The grounds are open from 12.00 noon to 5.00pm and the castle from 1.30pm to 4.30pm.

A free car park is situated on the A595 opposite the main gate, eight hundred yards from the castle. Disabled persons can park closer on request.

Most of the paths in the grounds are suitable for wheelchairs, as are the ground floor of the castle, the gift shop, the tearooms and the aviary.

Facilities: There are tearooms and toilets in the castle grounds; the staff are helpful. Details of admission fees can be obtained from the Estates Offices (0229 717614) or castle (0229 717203).

*Trail 9*
*Grade A*

# Broughton-in-Furness Town Trail

## *Starting Point*

Broughton is just off the main A595 Barrow to Workington road at the head of the Duddon estuary. There are magnificent views of the estuary and surrounding fells from the approach roads, but the village is in a sheltered hollow. The by-road from the east is twisty and narrow, and large vehicles should approach from the main road from the south (Foxfield), or the west down the steep hill from the High Cross Inn. Park in the square or nearby side streets.

## *Details of Trail*

You can join and leave this trail at any point depending on where you park, but our trail starts in the square which was built about 1760 when the lord of the manor returned from London, where squares had become fashionable. The town hall on the south side originally had open arches before the windows were added. There was a market here from 1125 until recently, and the right to hold a market still exists.

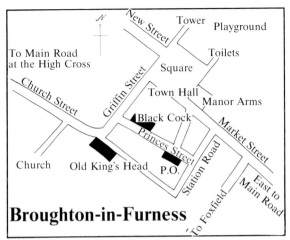

**Broughton-in-Furness**

To Main Road at the High Cross
New Street
Tower
Playground
Toilets
Square
Church Street
Griffin Street
Town Hall
Manor Arms
Black Cock
Princes Street
Market Street
Church
Old King's Head
P.O.
Station Road
Main Road
East to
To Foxfield

The obelisk erected in 1810 commemorates the Golden Jubilee of King George III, and the large chestnut trees were planted for Queen Victoria's Diamond Jubilee in 1897. The stocks are original stones with new timbers! In 1575 Elizabeth I granted a town charter to Broughton, and the charter proclamation is read from the steps of the obelisk on 1st August every year. Afterwards, pennies are thrown for the children, and everyone goes to the Old King's Head for a free half-pint and a 'fairing' cake.

In New Street there is a building with Gothic windows, called Gable Mount, built as a nursing home. Broom Hill nearby is handsome, but difficult to see safely.

Back in the square, turn right into Griffin Street, where some houses date back to 1672. On both sides of the street are archways into courtyards. Notice the bulges at the bottom of the house walls, where boulders are inset to prevent damage from cart wheels. When you reach Church Street, see Broughton House where Branwell Bronte, brother of the famous sisters, worked as a tutor in 1840, and the old advert for tobacco on the wall beside the shop nearby. Go past this to the church.

After a hundred yards, turn left at the converted school into a lane which leads (two hundred yards) to St. Mary Magdalen Church, which is part-Norman. Notice the marks on the doorposts where bowmen sharpened their arrows; a very old font; a church chest carved in oak and dated 1735; stained glass windows by Kempe; a 1595 bible; and a 'breeches' bible. A leaflet is available in the church.

Return to Church Street. If you can manage the steep slope, go past the Old King's Head, and if not, follow Prince's Street. At the end of these is the station building of the Furness to Coniston railway, closed in 1958 and now a house. Bank House, also now private property, was built as the Liverpool Bank.

Enter Prince's Street at the top or bottom to see the Wesleyan Chapel built in 1875. You can usually see a post-bus in Station Street or outside the post office and, if you have time, ride up the Duddon Valley with the local postman on his rounds (0730–12.30 delivery, 1645–1750 collection).

The old forge in Prince's Street is intact and can be visited by arrangement. Turn into Brade Street, or climb the steeper slope of Market Street past the garage, and go back towards the square, passing Kiln House, now the mountain centre.

Facilities: Radar key toilets just off the north-east corner of the square. Key may be borrowed from the Manor Arms Hotel in the square, or buy one from L. Brownrigg, St. Bees (0946) 822585; from your local Association for the Disabled; or from Radar, 25 Mortimer Street, London WIN 8AB (071-637-5400).

Refreshments: Manor Arms Hotel, The Square, Broughton-in-Furness, tel. (0229) 716282. One step entry, toilets in basement; Black Cock Inn, Prince's Street, Broughton-in-Furness, tel. (0229) 716529. Toilets not for wheelchairs, up steps; Old King's Head, Church Street, Broughton-in-Furness, tel: (0229) 716293. Toilets not for wheelchairs, up steps; High Cross Inn, off main road to west, tel. (0229) 716272. Lovely views. Ramp and two steps down to enter. Toilets not for wheelchairs, one step.

Mrs. Joan Morgan, Trail Advisor, tel. (0229) 716419, will guide tours by prior arrangement.

**Trail 10 Grade A**

# Dallam Deer Park and Kent Estuary Views

## Starting Point

Leave M6 northbound at junction 35 and take A6 to Milnthorpe, about 6½ miles. At the traffic lights in Milnthorpe turn left on to the B5282 (Arnside) and after about a mile there is a turning to the left (where there is a sign for Sandside). Park here where the side road is very wide, and the trail starts from here.

# Details of Trail

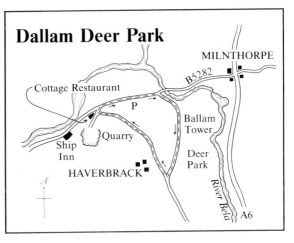

**Dallam Deer Park**

Two and a half miles on good surfaces, one hill with easy gradient.

Start by going along the B5282 towards Milnthorpe; the road can be rather busy, but there is a good footpath. In about five minutes you come to the entrance to the Dallam Estate on the right. Take this road (occasional cars), with the River Bela and its attractive bridge to your left and passing Dallam Tower to your right. Look out for the deer on the left. At the lodge turn right, with the small hamlet of Haverbrack ahead, and keep straight on along Lovers Lane. As you breast the hill there are views of Heversham and Milnthorpe to the right, and as you descend you have a magnificent view of the Kent Estuary and Lyth Valley with the Lakeland hills beyond. Turn right at the end of the lane, onto the quarry road, and you reach the car in about two hundred yards. By turning left onto the B5282 (footpath on opposite side of road) you come to the Cottage Restaurant in about two hundred yards, and there is a good view from the parking area opposite.

Facilities: Public toilets in The Square, Milnthorpe. Parking in square except Friday (market day).

Refreshments: The Cottage Restaurant, Sandside, Milnthorpe, tel: (05395) 63243. One small step at entrance. Access to toilets round the back to avoid steps; not very suitable. Serves lunches and dinners only, with afternoon teas in the high season. Restricted opening in winter. Excellent situation, good parking; The Lakelander Restaurant, The Square, Milnthrope, tel. (05395) 63829. One small step at entrance. Public toilets for disabled opposite side of square. Serves snacks and full meals. Open 9.00am to 9.00pm in season; in winter closed Thursdays and Tuesday afternoons; The Ship Inn, Sandside, tel. (05395) 63113. Shallow ramp at entrance. Toilets difficult. Serves good pub meals. Nice situation with good parking.

# Duddon Furnace Trail

## *Starting Point*

Broughton is just off the main A595 Barrow to Workington road at the head of the Duddon Estuary. There are magnificent views of the estuary and surrounding fells from the approach roads, but the village is in a sheltered hollow. The by-road from the east is twisty and narrow, and large vehicles should approach from the main road from the south (Foxfield), or the west down the steep hill from the High Cross Inn. Park in the square or nearby side streets to take advantage of Broughton's facilities.

Return to the main road at High Cross, turn right (signposted Workington A595, Millom 7) down the hill and across the valley to Duddon Bridge. After 150 yards, ignoring the left turn to Millom, carry straight on along Sign Fell Road for 125 yards and park inside the large gate on the left, where there is a hard-standing beside the path. Close the gate.

## *Details of Trail*

Go in along the public bridleway towards the old furnace. This was a working charcoal-fuel blast furnace from 1736 to 1867. The remains of the furnace are seen first, supported by modern steelwork, with the remains of the tail race (from the site of the undershot waterwheel) and the casting beds towards the road. Behind the furnace is the slope up which the barrows of ore, limestone and charcoal were pushed to fill the furnace from the top. Access off the track can be difficult, and you must take care on the grass slopes, but our 80-year-olds with sticks managed it

easily on a dry day. At the upper gate, see the ore store which is sealed off and used as a workshop at present. You can see the colour of the haematite by the stain low down on the front wall.

See how much bigger was the L-shaped charcoal store behind, because of the enormous bulk of this light-weight fuel. Stocks of ore would be built up all summer, and loads of charcoal carried down from the woodlands for miles around whilst the roads were dry. The furnace could only operate when there was a good flow in the river to

— 20 —

drive the bellows of the blast pumps – usually during the winter.

The neighbouring cottages, with running water at the door, were occupied until about 1960.

Total distance to the top of the site is 125 yards, rising 25 feet, plus explorations as you wish. The woodlands are very beautiful, but private.

Facilities in Broughton: Radar toilets just off the north-east corner of the square. Key may be borrowed from the Manor Arms Hotel in the square, or buy one from L. Brownrigg, St. Bees (0946) 822585; from your local Association for the Disabled; or from Radar, 27 Mortimer Street, London W1N 8AB (071-637-5400).

Manor Arms Hotel, The Square, Broughton-in-Furness, tel. (0229) 716286. One step at entry, toilets in basement; Black Cock Inn, Princess Street, Broughton-in-Furness, tel. (0229) 716529. Toilets not for wheelchairs, up steps; Old King's Head Hotel, Church Street, Broughton-in-Furness, tel. (0229) 716293. Toilets not for wheelchairs, up steps; High Cross Inn, off main road to west, tel. (0229) 716272. Lovely views. Ramp and two steps down to enter.

**Trail 12
Grade A**

# Circular Tour of Central Grange

## *Starting Point*

Leave M6 at junction 36, follow A590, signposted Barrow, for ten miles. At the roundabout at the bottom of Lindale Bypass, follow B5277 signposted Grange. After two miles enter Grange by the railway station and drive through along the promenade, arriving at Berners Close Hotel. The public car park is alongside the hotel.

# Details of Trail

Our walk begins at the Berners Close car park, near the fire station. There is a suitable toilet, a key to which can be obtained from the reception desk at Berners Close Hotel. A ramp at the hotel gives wheelchair access.

The walk lasts about an hour and has one steepish hill. It is circular, and about halfway round there are toilet facilities.

We begin by walking back from the car park to the main road. With Berners Close Hotel on the right, follow the pavement until a small lane is met which leads to the promenade. This is Clare House Lane. On the right is Berners Close, on the left Clare House. Move down the lane and onto the promande via the long, sloping bridge. This slope was built at the specific request of Col. Harold Porritt, a textiles director, at the beginning of this century, to allow bath-chair access. He certainly had vision! Harold Porritt also provided money for tearooms and shelters on the promenade. Opposite the tearooms was Clare House Pier, last used in 1910. The bandstand, again paid for by Harold Porritt, was sited here but because the ladies of Grange found smut-marks on their dresses from the nearby steam trains, it was moved to Park Gardens.

Walk along the promenade in the direction of the station until you reach the level crossing just after the playground. This is Bayley Lane, and in 1875 there was another pier here owned by the Morecambe Boat Company.

Heading towards the station you see on the left the upper storeys of the Commodore Hotel, which used to be the Bay Horse Coaching Inn, and the wall in front of the building was the old sea wall.

The railway was completed in 1857 at a cost of £360,000. There is access to the main road under the subway. A short push up will take you to the front of the station. The railway, masterminded by the Brog-den family, changed Grange into a commuter and tourist centre. Large houses were put up, and in 1866 the railway company built the Grange Hotel at a cost of £14,000. It also built gasworks, the stables, and a new station in 1872, and it started the first bus service.

Follow the pavement and enter the ornamental gardens opposite the large garage. Directly in front of you is England's tallest living tree to bear Christmas lights. The path leads you to the duck hut, in front of which is a small basin known as Picklefoot Spring, which is the original Grange well.

Note, please, that there are suitable toilet facilities here.

Continue to move out of the park with the small lake on your left, and cross the road. This is a longish push up the main street. On your left is the sunken garden, the approximate site of the granary from which Grange got its name. On your right is the building used as the district's first police station. All the buildings on Main Street are Grade 2 listed buildings.

At the top of Main Street, keep the Crown Hill Flats on the left-hand and the church on the right and travel down into the shopping area. The crossing could be fairly awkward. The church was completed in the early 1850s, and the clock tower was presented at precisely noon on the 12th December 1912, by Sophia Deardon.

Stop outside the Spar shop and look uphill. You will see a white building which is Hardcragg Hall, the oldest house in Grange and dated 1563.

Now cross the road on the Furness Building Society side and head along Kents Bank Road. You will pass several churches and the parish hall. The hall was for many older Grange residents the first educational establishment they attended. As you move further along the road, opposite the car park, you will see the British Legion premises. Until the early 1960s this was the National School, having been built some one hundred years earlier.

*Trail 13 Grade A*

# River Lune Walk

## *Starting Point*

Turn off the M6 at junction 34 taking the Kirkby Lonsdale road for approximately half a mile, then take the small slip road (signposted Halton) to the old railway station. Turn right into the car park. The walk starts here.

## Details of Trail

Walk along the old railway line towards Caton on the riverside to the Crook of Lune railway bridge (approximately one mile). There are toilets at this point. All gates allow room for wheelchairs. Return on the same route.

The walk is a nice pleasant one along the side of the River Lune. The pathways are in good condition and have a good surface, and there are many wild flowers along the way. You will often find canoeists using the rapids on this river, which is also good for bird-watching and for salmon.

Facilities: There are toilets in the car park at the Crook of Lune. There are also shops and public houses in the village of Caton nearby.

*Trail 14*
*Grade A*

# Williamson Park, Lancaster

## Starting Point

From Lancaster city centre take the road which passes the front steps of the town hall, up past the Lancaster Royal Grammar School. At the crossroads just past the school, turn right and continue uphill for a quarter of a mile, past the large park gates, and take the next turn left. You will see the car park ahead of you. (Buses from the city centre pass the Williamson Park gates.)

# Details of Trail

The walk commences on the footpath on the right hand side of the car park and follows the railings back to the main park gate. Turn right here into the wider drive and immediately you notice the rich variety of bushes, shrubs and trees on each side. Narrower paths lead off this main path, but keep straight ahead and pass the lake, which has been used by the Duke's Playhouse for scenes in outdoor promenade productions of Shakespeare, held each summer in various parts of the park.

A few minutes after passing the lake you will have your first sight of the hugely impressive 'folly', the Ashton Memorial. This unique monument is a familiar part of the landscape to Lancastrians and to those passing through the city by car or train. The vast memorial was commissioned at the beginning of this century by Lord Ashton, the linoleum millionaire and politician, as a monument to his family. The impressive steps climb up each side of the fountain to the first terrace, and then up again to the carved figures stretching upward to the huge copper dome with the observation tower on top.

Walking straight ahead, follow the wide path climbing steadily in front of you and, as it levels out, look to your left at the panorama of Lancaster with Morecambe bay in

the distance. At the end of the grassy area on your right, follow the path round to the right and head up towards the memorial building. (If this path is too steep there is a longer way round which follows the main wide pathway through the trees.)

We are now approaching the Butterfly House, which was originally the Palm House, and is well worth paying the admission fee to visit. Inside you will see a glorious variety of butterflies – free-flying, feeding and breeding – from Asia, Africa, Australasia and North and South America. The Butterfly

House is also a nursery, not only for rare and beautiful plants, shrubs and trees, but also for some of the more exotic and rarely-seen butterflies and moths, which can be bred throughout the year in considerable numbers. Refreshments and toilets are available in the building, and there is a shop selling postcards, etc., as mementoes of your visit.

Across in the main memorial building there is a permanent exhibition of photographs and displays from the Edwardian era depicting scenes of life in Lancaster, and particularly in James Williamson's (Lord Ashton's) factories on the banks of the Lune, where linoleum was produced and exported all over the world. There is wheelchair access both to this building and to the Butterfly House, and to the toilets.

On leaving these buildings, we walk to the right of the Butterfly House and start downhill past the lovely trees and rolling lawns with colourful plants in the borders on each side. Whatever the time of year, the gardeners manage to put on a fine display of shrubs and flowers. Go down the hill to the junction with the path we took on the way in, and turn left past the pond back to the car park.

A lovely and interesting walk of about one mile, away from traffic, with fine views and the added bonus of a visit to see the exotic butterflies.

Another place to visit that has wheelchair access, is the Maritime Museum on St. George's Quay on the riverside. Open all year round with cafe, gift shop and parking.

Facilities: Toilets and cafe by the Butterfly House.

## Trail 15 Grade A

# Surf, turf and scenic views

## *Starting Point*

Morecambe can easily be reached from several junctions on the M6, but if this is your first visit to Morecambe, junction 35 at Carnforth is the simplest exit point for this trail.

On leaving the M6 at junction 35, follow the signs for Morecambe, which will take you through Carnforth and along the coast to Morecambe; a distance of approximately seven miles.

# *Details of Trail*

The trail, three miles long, starts at the Happy Mount car park, which is on the approach to Morecambe and immediately adjacent to the golf course. It is a pay and display car park, and is well signposted.

From the car park, the route to the park is signposted. The park, which covers a level site, is well worth a visit for both the young and not-so-young. Disabled toilets are available there, along with the usual municipal park attractions, including a cafe. The Tourism Department organises events in the park during the summer months, with brass and silver bands being the principal attractions on Sunday afternoons. Telephone the Tourist Information Centre (0524 414110) for details.

On leaving the park by the front entrance, turn left and proceed along the landward side of the promenade to Prince's Crescent. This small local shopping parade, although on a slight incline, is worth a look. Refresh-ments can be had at either of two cafes on the crescent, or at two public houses.

Now back to the promenade, cross to the seaward side, turn left and proceed along to a fine vantage point opposite the town hall. This area incorporates a small children's play area. Of interest here is a plan depicting a panoramic view across Morecambe Bay, which is particu-larly interesting on a clear day, as all the Cumbrian Fells from Walney Island around to Ingleborough Fell in Yorkshire can be identified. This plan was presented by the Rotary Club of Morecambe and Heysham to commemorate the Rotary Golden Jubilee in 1955. Don't forget your binoculars, as adjacent to this is 'Birds of Morecambe Bay' display: very helpful in identifying the local birdlife. This display, also presented by Rotary, marks fifty years of service to the town.

Facilities are described in the text.

# Greenberfield Locks, Leeds/Liverpool Canal, Barnoldswick

## *Starting Point*

From the A59 (Gisburn/Skipton), approximately 1½ miles after leaving Gisburn, turn right onto the B6251 (signposted Barnoldswick). In approximately 2½ miles, turn left onto the B6252 (signposted Skipton 8½ miles). *After approximately half a mile, turn left into Coates Lane (immediately after a left-hand bend), and then after about another half-mile turn right into the car park.

Alternative route: From the A56 (Colne/Skipton), turn left in Kelbrook onto the B6383 (signposted Barnoldswick). In approximately 2¼ miles turn right on to the B6252 (signposted Skipton 8½). Then as from * above.

## *Details of Trail*

Leave car park and turn along lane. At fork, in approximately one hundred yards, turn right onto stone path. Bear right along canal towpath.

Note small red brick building with weir delivering water to the summit of the canal, at five hundred feet above sea-level. This is the outlet of a nine-mile conduit from a reservoir at Winterburn, near Gargrave. On the left is the lock-keeper's cottage, built in 1816. Note the sundial on the wall, commemorating the open-

ing of the diverted canal in 1824. The information board beyond the cottage provides further interesting details.

Through the gap in the towpath wall you can see the road bridge beyond the car park. The canal previously passed under this bridge via a stairway series of locks from near the cottage. Over-use of water necessitated alteration in the 1820s to the present system.

At the first lock, note the change

in water level. Pass under the bridge, taking care, as the original cobblestones are uneven, and noting the Ordnance Survey benchmark on the abutment. Beyond and to the right are the remains of the lime kiln.

At the second lock, pause and note a local geological feature. Ahead and to the right are many small conical hills. These are drumlins, caused by the glacial retreat at the end of the last Ice Age.

The short ramp beyond the third lock is where the 'new' canal channel meets the 'old'. Here the towpath becomes grassy but firm.

At the curve, note the modern chimney of the Rolls Royce aeroengine factory at Ghyll Brow, to your right. Ahead is a recently restored bridge previously used by horses crossing the canal where the towpath changes banks.

Wheelchairs cannot travel beyond here but, before retracing your steps, stop and admire the lovely open countryside.

At the third lock there is a short incline. You have a good view of the 'old' channel now used as an overflow. Between locks the old canal course is clearly visible, below and to the right, passing the white cottage. The old canal/road bridge has been converted into a stable!

Continue under the bridge (no. 157), again with care, and leave the towpath for the road, via a white gate. (The gate catch is a little difficult and assistance may be needed.) Turn left and return to the car park. Picnic benches and tables are available there.

Facilities: If you would like a closer look at the ancient St. Mary-le-Gill Church it is open Easter to September on Saturdays and Sundays from 2.00pm to 5.00pm Refreshments are available in the adjacent coach house. At other times the church can be opened by prior arrangement (tel: 813168). A toilet is available, but is unsuitable for wheelchair users.

The nearest public toilet is in the station car park (opposite the post office) in Barnoldswick town centre. No separate provision for the disabled, and only recommended for use in emergency.

The nearest restaurant/cafe is the Genevieve in Station Road, Barnoldswick, near the post office (tel: 0282 813572). Open every day; early closing Mondays and Tuesdays 3.00pm, and Wednesdays 2.00pm. One small step at entrance. Unisex toilet with narrow door, difficult for wheelchair users. Car park across from cafe. Staff helpful.

*Trail 17*
*Grade A*

# Ball Grove Recreation Centre, Cottontree, Colne

## *Starting Point*

Take the A6068 Colne/Keighley road and turn right to Trawden on the B6250; half a mile down the hill is Cottontree. At the fork in the road turn left by the fish and chip shop, following the sign for Ball Grove Recreation Centre, which is about a hundred yards on the left. Park by the adventure playground.

## Details of Trail

Walk along the bottom side of the playground area, following the stream on your right with the fishing lake on your left. About half a mile on this pathway, pass the white house to a gate. Retrace your steps, passing the picnic area on the right, until you come to a short bridge over a gulley. Follow the path round the lake to reach the toilets for the disabled, which are alongside the recreation room. The imposing building to your right is the Hide Restaurant.

Four fishing platforms have been constructed for disabled people, and fishing tackle is freely available from Pendle Leisure Services at Bank House, Albert Road, Colne. Tele-phone (0282) 865500 for further information about using the fishing tackle. The members of a local angling club have offered their help to any disabled person wishing to fish in the lake at Ball Grove.

The walking distance is about ¾ mile only, and takes forty minutes easy walking.

Facilities: Ball Grove Recreation Room overlooking the lake. The toilet for disabled people is at the end of the building and is accessible at all times; The Hide Restaurant; tel. (0282) 869117. Three steps. Staff will assist if necessary; Cottontree Inn, Winewall Road, Colne, tel. (0282) 863406; fish and chip shop, Cottontree.

**Trail 18
Grade A**

# Barley Picnic Area

## Starting Point

The car park, the starting point for this trail, is well signposted off the A6068 Padiham to Barrowford road, and is in the centre of Barley village, reached by three miles of narrow roads after leaving the A6068.

Barley is situated at the foot of Pendle Hill and, along with neighbouring villages of Newchurch-in-Pendle and Roughlee, is well known for its associations with the Pendle witches.

At the car park there are disabled toilets, and an information and refreshment cabin run by North West Water.

---

# Details of Trail

This trail of approximately two miles commences at the opposite end of the car park from the toilets etc. The walk is alongside Pendle Water on a level, unmade track through three gates, all unlocked. Starting through the hamlet of Narrowgate with its old mill converted into a private residence, and the renovated weavers' cottages, in just under one mile the next hamlet is Whithough with its 'camp school' on the hillside and Whithough Grange built in 1593. Turn right over the bridge and up the cobbled road (fifty metres at 1 in 7) to the main road. Before returning to Barley on the main road footpath, turn left over the brow of the hill to see Thorneyholme Square with the old cottages and, further down on the right, Thorneyholme Hall.

The route can be done in reverse according to preference of tackling the short steep section.

On return to Barley, a visit may be made to the village along the main road (without footpath). Alternative via picnic area does not allow access to village, owing to the narrow footbridge.

The trail is not very long, but combined with toilet facilities, refreshment hut and grassed picnic area with tables alongside Pendle Water, it is easy to pass at least half a day in the area.

Facilities: At the car park there are toilets for the disabled, an information centre and refreshment cabin. In the village there are several hotels, e.g. the Pendle Inn.

# Poulton-le-Fylde Urban Trail

## Starting Point

Park in Teanlowe car park, which is the best car park for handicapped/ disabled visitors, and has its own toilet facilities for the disabled.

## Details of Trail

1. To begin the tour of the ancient market town of Poulton-le-Fylde, stand on the steps of the parish church and look out over the **market place**. Poulton probably began life as a Saxon community, and its name means 'the town by the pool'; a reference to the River Wyre at Skippool.

2. Turn right into Church Street. On a shop wall opposite the church is a plaque marking the site of the **Plough Inn** which dated from the eighteenth century. The Plough Inn later became a house, and the original fireplace still stands at the front of the present shop.

3. Across the road stands the **Golden Ball**, dating from the eighteenth century, one of Poulton's three coaching inns. The archway was the entrance to the stabling at the back.

4. In 1896 the land at the back of the Golden Ball was developed as an **Auction Market**. Walk through the archway into what is now a car park. Attached to the brick walls surrounding the area can still be found traces of the iron rings to which bulls would be tethered on market days.

5. Stand outside the Golden Ball and look across the car park on the right. This is the site of an ancient **tithe barn**.

6. Looking to the right, in the distance can be seen the original building of the Independent Chapel, now the United Reform Church. It was restored in 1886, and now serves as the church hall.

7. Look carefully at the shops just past the Golden Ball and you will see that the buildings were once two fine houses. Parts of the original doorways still stand.

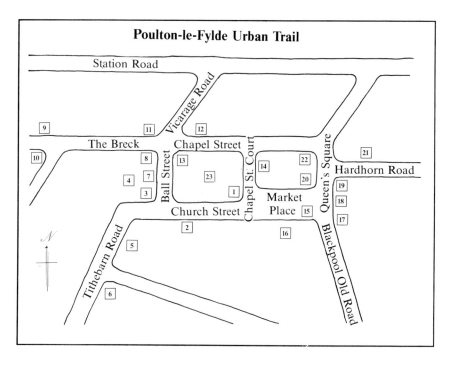

## Poulton-le-Fylde Urban Trail

Station Road

Vicarage Road

The Breck    Chapel Street

Chapel St. Court

Ball Street

Church Street

Market Place

Queen's Square

Hardhorn Road

Blackpool Old Road

Tithebarn Road

*N*

8. Walk to the corner of Ball Street and turn left into The Breck. The white building on the left was the birthplace of **William Thornber**, a noted local historian.

9. Continue a little way down The Breck to the **railway station**. The first line to Poulton was opened in 1840 and the original station stood at the bottom of Breck Road. The present station was built in 1894 and has one of the longest platforms in England.

10. Look down **The Breck** and notice the large Victorian houses built in the 1880s by wealthy businessmen who came to live in Poulton from all over Lancashire. A back street runs behind the houses, and the outbuildings were originally built as stabling.

11. Walk back towards the church. The building on the left, immediately next to the railway bridge, was a smithy in the 1840s and the older shops on both sides of The Breck were originally thatched cottages and workshops. On the corner of The Breck and Vicarage Road is the Conservative Club, until 1929 **The Ship Inn**, which accounts for the sailing ships to be seen high up on the brick walls.

12. Look across Vicarage Road to a fine detached house on the corner of Chapel Street. It was built as the

town **savings bank** in 1839, the date marked by a plaque on the end wall.

13. The present pub, known as **The Thatched House**, was erected in 1910 and replaced an ancient cruck-built inn which stood at right angles to this one. Because parishioners often had long distances to travel to church, pubs were often built next to the church.

14. Walk down Chapel Street and just past the Thatched House, turn right into Chapel Street Court. This was once notorious as **Potts Alley** with lodging houses on either side and an open drain down the centre. Walk to the marketplace-end of the old wall, and look closely at the old brickwork and you will see the original front doorsteps of these houses.

15. Leave Chapel Street Court and walk into Market Place where you will see the **market cross, stocks, whipping post and fish slab**. The lamp post was erected to commemorate Queen Victoria's Golden Jubilee in 1887.

16. On the west side of the **market place** stands a long three-storey terrace of shops. A plaque commemorates the burning-down in 1732 of the thatched medieval cottages.

17. Turn away from the church and notice a row of three buildings overlooking the stocks. The **Bull Hotel** remains but has a modern front. This was another of Poulton's coaching inns.

18. **Alexander Rigby's house** –

the National Westminster Bank replaced a fine three-storey town house built in 1692 by Sir Alexander Rigby of Layton Hall.

19. **James Baines' house** – a wool merchant who lent money to local inhabitants, rather like a building society does today. His house has been little altered on the outside, and is a good example of Georgian handmade brickwork.

20. Turn left out of the marketplace and into **Queen's Square** (known as 'Workhouse Square' in the eighteenth century). The three-storey building on the left was Poulton's third coaching inn, the **Spread Eagle**. A little further on, the frieze depicting the four seasons over the archway is a reminder of the **corn mill** which stood behind this building until the late 1960s. The oldest remaining cobblestones in Poulton can be seen in this passageway.

21. Cross Queen's Square and walk a little way down Hardhorn Road, once known as 'Wheatsheaf Street', after a pub which stood here. Some of Poulton's oldest cottages are here. On the right-hand side was the house of **Samuel Lomas**, a well known clockmaker in the eighteenth century. The building at the corner of Queen's Square and Hardhorn Road was built as Poulton's Institute in the early 1900s to provide activities for the young people of the town.

22. Walk back into Queen's

Square and continue to the corner of Chapel Street. On the opposite corner is a terrace of small cottages typical of those found in eighteenth-century Poulton. The road leading away from Queen's Square is known as Higher Green, and further on becomes Lower Green.

23. Walk back up Chapel Street to the entrance to St. Chad's church-yard and cross the churchyard to the fascinating **parish church**, which is usually open during daylight hours. It is well worth a visit to complete your tour of Poulton-le-Fylde.

Facilities: There are toilets for the disabled in the Teanlowe car park. The following is a list of cafes and restaurants where meals can be obtained: The Coffee Pot, 4 Queen's Square; The Cornmill, Chapel Street Court; The Mews Salad and Sandwich Bar, 7 Chapel Street Court; Marples in The Village Walks (part of the Teanlowe Centre); New Penny Grill, 4a Tithebarn Street; Liberty's by the Park, Vicarage Road.

An illustrated pamphlet, giving far more details of the town trail, is

available from: Long's Bookshop (by the side of St. Chad's Church); The Cornmill, Chapel Street; The Village Newsagents, Market Square; New Penny (next to New Penny Grill); R. & B. Duckworth (news-agents), 9 Breck Road; Out and About, 25 Breck Road.

# Towneley Park

## *Starting Point*

Towneley Hall is signposted with a brown tourist sign off the A67, Todmorden Road, just out of the town centre on the south side of Burnley. Drive for one mile along the main approach, where you will find ample parking in front of the hall. You will find the trail on O.S. Pathfinder Map, Burnley, sheet SD 83/93.

## *Details of Trail*

Towneley Hall was completed in the fifteenth century although, since 1600, there have been extensive alterations. If you wanted to visit the hall as part of your walk, it would be advisable to telephone so that a

member of staff could be on hand to assist. The hall is now the home of an impressive art gallery and museum although, unfortunately, wheelchair users only have access to the ground floor.

There are many things to do and see in this, Burnley's largest park. There is a craft museum with ramped access. The Old Stables Cafe with level, but cobbled, access and plenty of space for wheelchairs. The Natural History Centre has a 'minibeasts' area, as well as a geological garden, and, next to the centre, is the bowling green which is a hive of activity in the warm months.

Much of the park is accessible to wheelchairs, as many of the paths have tarmac surfaces with shallow gradients. The nature trail behind Towneley Hall in the southern part of the park has steep paths which are accessible only to the very determined, but the Thanet Lee Wood Trail has virtually level stone paths with the occasional tree root. If you were particularly eager to explore the southern nature trail and eliminate steeper gradients, you could park at the park entrance opposite the lay-by, two kilometres south of the main entrance. This would be essential for users of self-propelled wheelchairs, as these chairs aren't designed for such gradients.

There are many picnic tables near the hall, with numerous benches scattered around the park. There are disabled toilets both inside the hall and outside.

The suggested route covers two kilometres of tarmac path and traffic-free boulevard. Allow half a day for the trail.

Facilities are mentioned in the text.

The telephone number of Towneley Hall is (0282) 24213.

# Stanah Riverside Trail, Thornton

## Starting Point

Leave the M55 at junction 3 and take the A585 towards Fleetwood. Continue along the A585 for 6½ miles until you reach the roundabout at the River Wyre Hotel, then take the third exit (B5412). Follow signposts for Stanah Picnic Site. The trail starts from the car park furthest from the main entrance.

## Details of Trail

The trail runs alongside the River Wyre for approximately five hundred metres and affords extensive views over the estuary and saltmarsh. The surface is compacted limestone and is suitable for wheelchairs. A tapping rail has been installed for the visually handicapped. The trail is

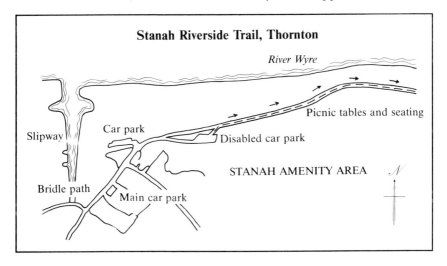

**Stanah Riverside Trail, Thornton**

River Wyre

Picnic tables and seating

Slipway

Car park

Disabled car park

STANAH AMENITY AREA

Bridle path

Main car park

linear, not circular, and leads to two picnic tables with seating. A future extension to the trail is envisaged, along with interpretative material and more site furniture. The area is especially popular with sailing enthusiasts and bird watchers.

Facilities: The nearest toilets suitable for wheelchair users are at the Teanlowe Centre, Poulton and in the shopping precinct at Thornton. NB: Toilet facilities to be on site in the near future.

Nearest hotels, cafes, public houses accessible by wheelchairs are: Thornton Lodge, Skippool Road, Thornton, tel. (0253) 882455. Restaurant and bar; River Wyre Hotel, Breck Road, Poulton, tel. (0253) 883791. Restaurant and bar; Mains Hall Hotel, Mains Lane, Poulton, tel. (0253) 885130. Accommodation; Kneps Farm Caravan Park, River Road, Cleveleys, tel. (0253) 823632. Caravans and cafe.

*Trail 22
Grade A*

# The Park and St. Bartholomew, Great Harwood

## *Starting Point*

Take the A680 from Accrington towards Whalley. Turn left (signposted Great Harwood) opposite Nightingale's Garage. Travel along Harwood New Road, Harwood Lane. The Park public house is on the right about half a mile from the A680. The trail starts here.

# Details of Trail

Turn right from the car park and follow the road uphill for about fifty yards to Allsprings Drive. Turn right into Allsprings Drive. You are now travelling on the original carriage drive to 'Allsprings', the home of the Lord of the Manor, James Lomax (1803-1886). Carry straight on past the playing fields on the left and take in the magnificent views towards Pendle on the right. At the end you will see the old gatehouse of Allsprings, a lovely little building dating from 1838. Turn left and in a few yards turn right and take the path into the memorial Park. This land was bought from Mrs. Trappes Lomax in 1920 by three local men, James Boardman, William Pickup and Henry Milton Thompson who, on the 25th July 1920, conveyed the land to the Urban District Council as a gift, to make a public park for ever. Carry on up this path a little way and you will come to a small brick building which houses a small aviary, mostly budgerigars. As this park is built on a hillside you may care to stay and enjoy the lower end of the park and take a look at the war memorial in the Garden of Remembrance. The obelisk made from Creetown granite is imperishable and highly polished. The memorial was unveiled on 2nd October 1926 by Major General Sir Neil Malcolm, KCB. DSO, assisted by Mrs Ormerod of Great Harwood, who lost three sons in the war. Leave the park by the path further along towards the church.

When you reach the church you may care to take a look inside (this will not always be possible as, sadly, it is very often locked). St. Bartholomew was first mentioned in a document dated 1335 in which it was described as 'the chapel of Harwood'. It would have been a simple structure, built as a chapel-of-ease and served either from Blackburn or the very new Whalley Abbey. It was dedicated originally to St. Lawrence, but no-one knows when the change of dedication to St. Bartholmew took place.

The oldest part of the present building is the tower, dated sometime in the fifteenth century. Against the tower arch can be seen the pitch of an earlier, steeper nave roof.

After leaving the church, return up Church Lane and turn right into Brantfell Road. Some of the very large houses on your right were built by local millowners. At the bottom of Brantfell Road, turn right and once again you join Allsprings Drive. Carry on until you reach the main road and turn left back to The Park public house.

Facilities: The Park Public House, Park Lane, Great Harwood, tel. (0254) 886080. Bar snacks 12 noon to 2pm daily. Entrance two shallow steps. Toilets: ladies very good, wide doors, access reasonable; gents next to ladies not too good for access, better to use toilets through the pool room; The Game Cock Public House, on A680, five hundred yards from Nightingale's Garage. tel: (0254) 883719. Purpose-built disabled toilets here.

## Trail 23 Grade A

# Witton Park Visitor Centre, Blackburn

## Starting Point

On the right of the A674 Blackburn to Chorley/Preston road (Preston Old Road), 1½ miles from the town centre. Situated in Witton Country Park, opposite the Scapa factory. Car park just inside entrance on right. Disabled allowed to drive their vehicles up to the Visitor Centre.

## Details of Trail

From the car park continue up main walk past the athletics arena on the right. The Visitor Centre is clearly marked past the cafe. The courtyard of the centre is cobbled and could present slight difficulty for some wheelchairs.

The Visitor Centre contains restored stable and coach-houses with a display of farm machinery. There are also changing exhibitions in one of the rooms (see local press for details). A wildlife corner is in the course of development adjacent to the centre.

On leaving the centre, turn left at path through line of trees towards lily pond on left. Take path on right towards cafe and back to car park round athletics arena.

Opening times: Thursday, Friday, Saturday 1–5pm; Sunday and Bank Holidays 11–5pm (except Christmas and New Year). Tel: (0254) 55423.

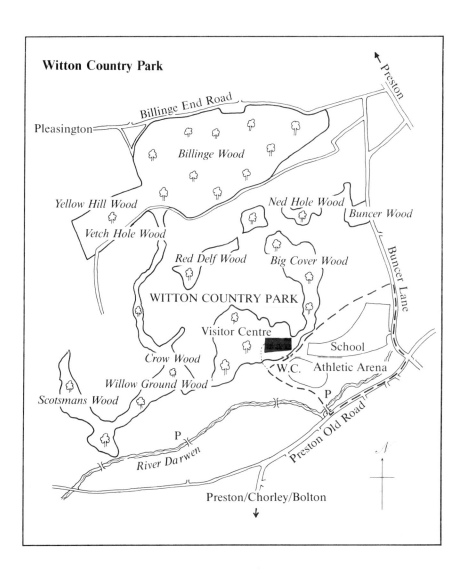

This map refers to Trails 23 and 24.

# Witton Country Park
# and St. Mark's, Blackburn

## Starting Point

From Blackburn town centre take the A674 Preston and Chorley road. After two miles look for the Scapa Porritt works on the left. Turn right into Witton Park and park the car. Disabled toilets here (sometimes locked).

## Details of Trail

Note: This walk is an extension of Trail 23.

Proceed on tarmac road towards visitor centre. Through open parkland and past children's adventure play area. (Note running track on right.) Picnic tables on parkland. Turn right towards cafe then onto tarmac path through the trees (toilets in cafe). At first junction turn left and go through gate to lily pond, return to main path and turn left through gate to car park. Straight on up tarmac path or turn left up stone track which rejoins main tarmac path at the top of slope near school. At main road (Buncer Lane) note coat of arms above door to St. Mark's Church. Turn right down hill to traffic lights, right again to starting point. On entering Witton Park note the meeting of the Rivers Darwen and Blakewater.

Distance 1¾ miles, time one hour.

Good paths, no steep or hard sections.

# Preston Dock

## Starting Point

Access from the south or west (south of the Ribble) via the A582 and A59 eastbound. First left on Strand Road.

Access from south or east (through town centre) via A59 westbound. Right at the bottom of Fishergate Hill on to Strand Road, then first left.

Access from west (north of the Ribble) and north via the A583 (Blackpool Road).

## Details of Trail

Preston Dock was opened in the 1890s and closed as a commercial dock in the early 1970s. After several years' delay, major re-development of the dock site – extending to several hundred acres – began in the mid-1980s. Building of both commercial and residential properties is now proceeding apace and many well known organisations have located there. Visitors could spend an interesting afternoon compiling a list and awarding each participant marks on the correct names recorded.

It is suggested that visitors use the car park at the north-west corner of the harbour basin. The car park is on the harbour edge. If this small car park is full, there are large car parks across the road at Texas Home Care or Morrison's.

There is a level promenade (Grade A surface) stretching to the swing bridge at the entrance to the basin from the river. The promenade is about eight hundred yards in length.

A marina for yachts and pleasure craft is being developed and moorings have been created at the west end of the basin.

At the western end of the lighted promenade, The Waterfront (a 'Toby Grill') has been opened and food is available at the bar or in the restaurant. Access presents no difficulties and there is a toilet for the disabled.

There are also small cafes in both Texas Home Care and in Morrison's 26-checkout supermarket. Toilets for the disabled are available in both places. Incidentally, Morrison's sell major brands of petrol at low prices.

Also on the dock site is a MacDonald's and a ten-screen cinema, ideal for children's birthday outings. Both have spacious car parks. When walking eastwards along the waterside promenade one has a panoramic view of the Preston skyline.

Facilities mentioned in text.

*Trail 26
Grade A*

# Hurst Park, Penwortham

## *Starting Point*

Access from the A59 and Hill Road, a cul-de-sac leading off the A59. For visitors driving eastward, Hill Road is the first road on the right after going through the traffic lights at the junctions of Priory Lane and Cop Lane with the Liverpool road.

For westbound traffic, Hill Road is the second road on the left, after crossing Penwortham Bridge at the foot of Fishergate.

It is suggested that cars are parked in the section of Hill Road just beyond the entrance to Hurst Park and the junction with Valley Road.

## *Details of Trail*

Walking towards the end of Hill Road one will see a stile* on the right hand side of the road. A four-hundred-yard long Grade A surface path runs from here to a second stile* which in turn leads to: a) a pedestrian bridge over the Penwortham Bypass in the direction of Hill Road South, and b) a Grade A surface path running along, but well above, the bypass to Cop Lane. A distance of about five hundred yards.

There are two Grade B surface paths forking to the right of the section between the two stiles referred to above. These paths converge by a pond, and go on to meet the path running parallel with the bypass. Near the junction of these paths there is a second bridge over

the bypass leading to Hill Road South.

There are three small ponds in the area described, and one sees children with nets and fishing rods.

Whilst walking along the main section one has splendid elevated panoramic views of the Preston skyline, with a backdrop of the Longridge Fells.

To enter Hurst Park one should retrace one's steps to the park gates opposite Valley Road, a distance of less than two hundred yards from the first stile mentioned above. There is an undulating Grade A surface drive from Hill Road to Cop Lane – a distance of about five hundred yards

– passing through the centre of the park. Attractive flowerbeds are planted in season and there is a well-equipped children's playground. Low grade toilets are located in the centre of the park.

Good bar meals are available at the Fleece Inn on Liverpool Road, at the junction with Cop Lane. One could leave the car park, cross the road and walk up Cop Lane to the Fleece and return after having taken refreshments. There is a large car park at the Fleece should you prefer to use it.

\* denotes that the stile is designed to enable a person in a wheelchair to negotiate it without difficulty.

*Trail 27*
*Grade A*

# Britannia Greenway, Bacup

## *Starting Point*

Approximately 1½ miles south of Bacup on the A671, just after the junction with the A6066 (New Line) there is a petrol station on the right, followed by a row of cottages, then the car park.

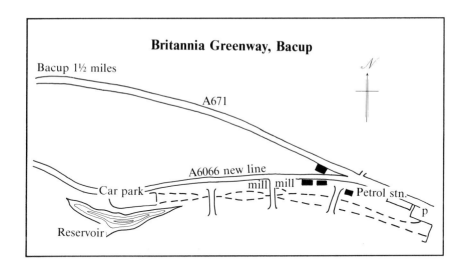

## Britannia Greenway, Bacup

Bacup 1½ miles

A671

A6066 new line

Car park

mill mill

Petrol stn.

p

Reservoir

*Details of Trail*

The trail leaves the car park. It is a recently constructed trail over the old railway line, now a bridleway and suitable for wheelchairs.

The trail is ¾ mile long, with a car park at each end. Alternatively, walkers may wish to do the return journey.

Facilities: There are disabled toilets in Bacup town centre or Stacksteads car park (two miles west). Both are locked at 6.30pm.

# Cowm Reservoir Trail, Whitworth

## *Starting Point*

Travel on the A671 for approximately three miles south of Bacup towards Rochdale. Pass the Whitworth Civic Hall on the right and turn right into Tong Lane. Carry on up to Cowm Reservoir car park.

## *Details of Trail*

The trail has been prepared by Rossendale Groundwork and the North West Water Authority. It is a circular trail of approximately 1½ miles round the reservoir. The surface was loose chippings, but should be improved by the time this book is published.

Facilities: There are temporary toilets for the disabled on the car park. Renewed disabled toilets are at Healey Corner, one mile south on the A671.

**Cowm Reservoir Trail**

Bacup 3 miles

Cowm Park Way

A671

Whitworth
Civic Hall

*Cowm Reservoir*

Car park

Tong Lane

Tong End

Rochdale 4 miles

# Irwell Valley Way

## Starting Point

The Groundwork Countryside Centre is about half a mile west of Rawtenstall town centre. From the roundabout proceed on the A56 to Bury, for approximately two hundred yards. J.A. Taylor, Ford dealers' showrooms on the right. Immediately past, and before the bridge, turn right into New Hall Hey Road. Continue to the end. The car park and Groundwork Centre are at the end of New Hall Hey Road.

Motorway access to Rawtenstall is via the M66 from the south leading to the A56/A682 Rawtenstall–Edenfield bypass; from the north by the A56 from the M65.

## Details of Trail

The multi-purpose Groundwork Countryside Centre is based in mid-nineteenth-century converted farm buildings, with an attractive riverside location at New Hall Hey, Rawtenstall. Overlooking the site is the splendid renovated facade of Hardman's Mill, a masterpiece of Victorian architecture. Surrounded by the Rossendale hills, the centre is a natural focal point for walkers and countryside enthusiasts.

A wide range of attractions is on offer, including:
— The Penguin Visitor Centre with a changing programme of displays and special events.
— Shop selling a range of specialist publications, maps and craft items.
— Cafe serving an extensive range of herbal and other teas, coffee, biscuits and home-made cakes.
— Information on Rossendale and surrounding countryside attractions.
— The Doorstep Fresh Farm Centre with a permanent exhibition of farming in the Pennines.
— Attractive natural stone picnic tables situated on the banks of the River Irwell.
— Free car parking and free admission.

The trail starts from the picnic area at the Groundwork Centre and then proceeds along the river's edge for five hundred yards or more and then returns to the picnic area. Toilets and cafe at the picnic area

— 51 —

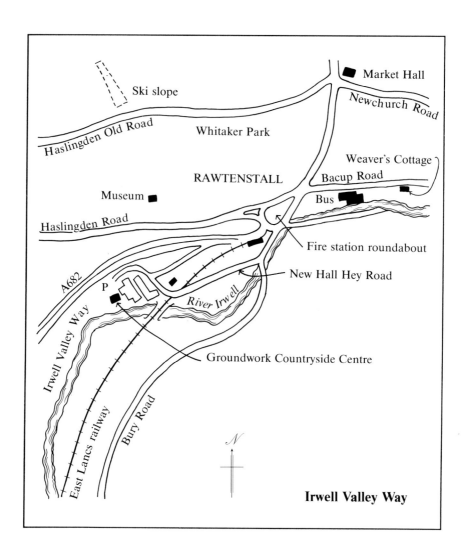

Market Hall

Newchurch Road

Ski slope

Haslingden Old Road

Whitaker Park

Weaver's Cottage

RAWTENSTALL

Bacup Road

Museum

Bus

Haslingden Road

Fire station roundabout

New Hall Hey Road

A682

P

River Irwell

Irwell Valley Way

Groundwork Countryside Centre

Bury Road

East Lancs railway

N

**Irwell Valley Way**

with plenty of seating facilities.

Points of interest: wild flower garden; model town centre; fishing in the river; some wild ducks etc.; large wooden bridge; Penguin Visitor Centre with changing programme of events; shop selling maps and craft items; Doorstep Fresh Farm Centre.

Facilities mentioned in the text.

— 52 —

# Anglezarke Woodland Trail, near Chorley

## Starting Point

The trail starts at Anglezarke car park, south-east of Chorley. Take the A6 south through Chorley, turn left to Adlington and left up Babylon Lane to Rivington. Pass over the motorway and take the left turn to Anglezarke.

## Details of Trail

Leave the car park and walk down to Anglezarke Reservoir. Here you enter the park. The tarmacadam path goes by the reservoir. There is then an incline up to High Bullough Reservoir on the right. Eventually you come to a locked gate, and this is as far as wheelchairs can go. Retrace your steps and eventually you will return to a left hand fork. Take this path up to a viewing point. This carries on to the car park.

Facilities: None in the park.

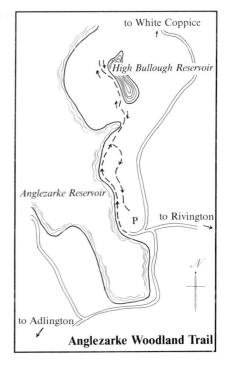

to White Coppice

High Bullough Reservoir

Anglezarke Reservoir

to Rivington

P

to Adlington

N

**Anglezarke Woodland Trail**

— 53 —

# Force Crag Mine, Coledale, Cumbria

## Starting Point

Leave the M6 at junction 40 (Keswick/Penrith) and take the A66 to Keswick. Keep on the A66 past Keswick (or if in Keswick take the B5259 out of Keswick) in the direction of Cockermouth and Workington. Turn left at the B5259 signposted Whinlatter/Lorton. Follow this road into the village of Braithwaite and keep to the Whinlatter/Lorton signs past the Royal Oak public house. The road narrows here through the village and then climbs past the sign for the Coledale Inn. Continue up the hill, ignoring the footpath sign to the left, to the car park.

## Details of Trail

This walk is linear, not circular, and covers four miles.

Leave the car park, taking the gravel track. The first part of the walk rises steadily and has many wheel tracks to negotiate. Continue on through the gate, still rising. After about ¾ mile the path levels off and becomes much smoother. Stop on your ascent and look back at the lovely view of Braithwaite Village with Keswick in the distance and Skiddaw in the background. Also, for the duration of the walk you will hear the noisy babble of Coledale Beck below you in the valley.

The walk can be terminated at any length, but is two miles to Force Crag Mine and the view of Grizedale Pike on the right, Grasmoor straight ahead, with Outerside on the left, and Causey Pike in the background.

At the end of the valley you should see the waterfalls into Coledale Beck. The hills on either side can make this walk very windy, but after the first rise it is fairly level and easy to negotiate.

Before or after you walk you can continue up the road from the car park to a lay-by on the right where, on a clear day, there is a beautiful view of Bassenthwaite Lake and Skiddaw. Further on still, up the same road, is the Whinlatter Visitor Centre where details of forest walks and trails can be obtained.

Facilities: There are toilets at the Derwent Water Hotel, Portinscale, but these are not ideal for wheelchairs. Best to use the disabled toilets in the central car park in Keswick. National key scheme, or borrow key from Information Centre, Moothall, Keswick.

Refreshments can be obtained from: Derwent Water Hotel, Portinscale, tel. Keswick 72538. Level entrance, toilets not ideal for wheelchairs. Staff helpful, bar or restaurant food; Royal Oak, Braithwaite, tel. Braithwaite 533. Level entrance, good bar lunches, real ale. Toilets not ideal for wheelchairs. Many others in Keswick town centre.

Trail 32
Grade B

# Friar's Crag Nature Walk, Keswick

## Starting Point

The route starts at the National Trust Information Centre at the boat landing (GR 265229). Parking and toilets are by the Keswick Theatre.

## Details of Trail

The original route is a circular one of approximately 2¼ miles (3.6kms) laid out for wheelchairs by the National Trust. There are no hills, but it can be slippery and muddy after rain. The walk includes the magnificent views across Derwent Water and particularly towards Borrowdale.

From the National Trust Information Centre follow the tarmac road before taking the path to

Friar's Crag. Wheelchairs must back-track for a few yards from the crag before following the route towards Ings Woods. For the majority, a return from Brocklebeck is advised, but a strong and determined pusher can achieve a longer route past Stable Hills to Broom Plant. Half way round Calfclose Bay follow the path into Great Wood. This runs parallel to the Borrowdale road. Opposite Castle Head (the plug of an old volcano) the path turns left. Here are both steep steps and a ramp before the path goes through Cockshott Woods to the Information Centre. All gates and bridges on the route are negotiable.

The walk can be extended to the Borrowdale road at GR 271223, to make it a five-mile (8km) return route.

Facilities: There are toilets by the Keswick Theatre, and a lakeside tearoom and toilets near the car park.

Note: This walk was taken from the booklet *Access to the Countryside for Wheelchair Users*.

**Trail 33
Grade B**

# Kirkby Stephen/Hartley Circular Trail

## Starting Point

The trail starts in the market square in the centre of Kirkby Stephen.

## Details of Trail

Leave the market square via the main road heading north. Take a right fork into Hartley Road and cross the bridge over the River Eden. On crossing the bridge, turn right and continue to the village of Hartley. At the junction in the village turn left and continue until the road forks. Take the left hand fork into Slackgap Lane and turn left at the next junction. This is Kirkbank Lane. As you proceed you will see Eden Place on your left, where there are free-flying parakeets. At the main road, bear left. On the opposite side of the road there is a nursery and garden centre. Follow the main road back into Kirkby Stephen.

Eighty per cent of the trail is on quiet country lanes, and for the remainder of the trail there is a footpath.

Facilities: There are toilets for the disabled in the market square in Kirkby Stephen, and there are cafes and a public house in the town centre.

Further details of this trail can be obtained from: Colin Littlefair, Insurance & Investment Consultant, Market Square, Kirkby Stephen, tel. (07683) 71961.

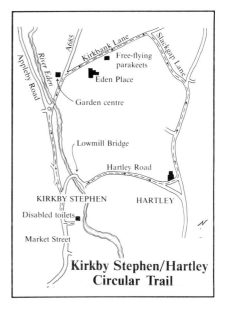

**Kirkby Stephen/Hartley Circular Trail**

# Rothay Valley and Rydal Park Trail, Ambleside

## *Starting Point*

The starting point of the trail is St. Mary's Parish Church, Ambleside. The church is situated close to the centre of the town.

# Details of Trail

The trail covers a distance of 3½ miles.

Follow the footpath into St. Mary's churchyard and then turn right to emerge on to a surfaced road. Turn left along this road, passing Ambleside C. of E. Junior School, and then through a gate into Rothay Park. At the entrance to the park there are public conveniences with disabled persons' facilities and ramped access for wheelchairs.

From the road through the park there is a fine view northwards (to the right) across to Low Pike. The road eventually leads over two bridges in quick succession, the first one crossing Stock Ghyll and the second the River Rothay as it flows south from Rydal Water to Windermere.

Immediately after crossing the second bridge, turn right on to a tarmacadamed minor road following the River Rothay. The road skirts the eastern slope of the fell known as Loughrigg to the left, while looking across the River Rothay to the right, and also to the rear, there are fine views of Ambleside and Wansfell. (If a rest is required, a wooden seat can be found on the left hand side of the road approximately half a mile from the bridge over the Rothay.) Watch out for the picturesque stepping stones across the river.

Eventually the minor road itself crosses the River Rothay at Pelter Bridge, to emerge on to the main A591 trunk road. Here turn left and proceed along the footpath adjacent to the A591 for approximately four hundred yards, before crossing the road at the first right turn, where signs indicate Rydal Hall and Rydal Mount. Note that the A591 can be extremely busy with traffic, and great care will be needed when crossing.

If refreshments and/or toilets are required, there is a public house a couple of hundred yards further along the A591, but afterwards it will be necessary to retrace your steps to the junction.

Rydal Mount was the home of William Wordsworth from 1813 until his death in 1850, and is open to visitors.

There is a steep uphill climb away from the A591 for about 150 yards before you take the second turning on the right onto a wide stony track. This track passes alongside Rydal Hall and over Rydal Beck where, from the bridge, the stream can be seen cascading down over picturesque waterfalls.

Within the grounds of Rydal Hall there is a sign indicating the direction of the footpath to Ambleside, and the wide track passes between tall evergreen trees.

The track continues through

Rydal Park, and although two large wooden gates provide obstructions, they are never locked and are easily opened to allow passage through. The views from Rydal Park are beautiful in all directions.

The track eventually emerges on to the main A591, where you must turn left and proceed for approximately one mile back to the centre of Ambleside. (Remember, again, that great care is needed when crossing this busy road.)

Facilities: There are toilets and refreshments in Ambleside, and facilities on the walk itself are mentioned in the text.

# Escape to Eskdale by the 'Ratty', Ravenglass

## Starting Point

Leave the M6 at junction 36 and follow the signposts to Barrow. Take the A590 to Greenodd and then the A595 to Ravenglass. Here one should catch the train. There are regular trains with facilities for wheelchairs, but it is better to confirm accommodation in advance by telephoning (0229) 717171.

## Details of Trail

Distance: return Dalegarth to Boot, one mile. This can be extended.

The 'Ratty' is England's oldest narrow gauge railway, hauling passengers for seven miles from the sea at Ravenglass Estuary to the rugged grandeur of some of England's highest hills.

From coaches that suit the weather and which can be adapted to take wheelchairs, you are likely to see waders on the marshes, buzzards over Raven Crag, and roe deer anywhere up the line.

Including Ravenglass, the starting point, and Dalegarth, the terminus, there are six stations in all, and you can stop off at any one of these to experience the changing beauty of the Eskdale Valley. Recommended stops are Ravenglass and Dalegarth,

where all required facilities are available.

Ravenglass was named *Clanoventa* by the Romans, and today the small, attractive estuary village is the home of the Ravenglass and Eskdale Railway with its station, workshops, pub and museum. A wander through the village will be enjoyable.

From Dalegarth, it is a gentle walk to Boot village where there are numerous sights of interest and beauty. The distance is about half a mile on a country road. For the more energetic, it is possible to continue on the road after Boot, as far as the Wool Pack Inn. You must remember, however, that you have to make the return journey to Dalegarth by the same route, to catch the train back to Ravenglass.

Facilities: At Ravenglass, Irton Road and Dalegarth stations. The Irton Road toilet is normally locked, and the driver/guard has the key.

Refreshments: Ratty Arms, Ravenglass Station; Dalegarth Station Cafe and Shop; Ravenglass Station Cafe and Shop.

**Trail 36 Grade B**

# Lune Linear Walk, Lancaster

## Starting Point

At the Lancaster end of the walk, the car park is off the A683 north of its junction with the A6. This walk is an extension of Trail 13.

## Details of Trail

The linear park was established several years ago on land owned by North West Water between Lancaster and Horbrook o' Lune, on the former railway line. It is about four miles in length, and its stoned surface is ideally suited for wheelchairs. Kissing gates at various points on the route have been deliberately designed with wheelchairs in mind. There is a car park at the Crook o' Lune end of the walk, and another on the site of the old Halton Station in Halton village. Access to the walk can be made from any of these car parks.

Facilities: Toilets are constructed on the car parks at each end of the walk. There are no cafes on the route, but there are public houses and shops in Lancaster, Halton and Caton.

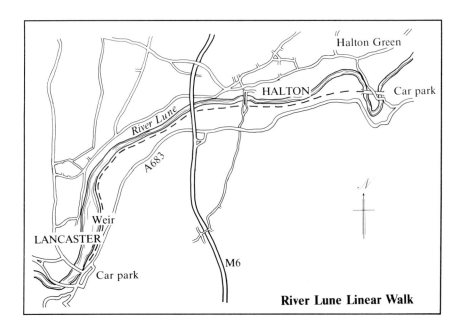

Trail 37
Grade B

# 'Nicky Nook', near Garstang

## *Starting Point*

Travelling north on the A6 from Preston, pass the Garstang exit and then on towards Scorton via Gubberford Lane (signposted Scorton). Pass under the railway after about two miles, then take the first right, by the bowling green, and go under the M6 motorway. At the T-junction turn right, and after two hundred yards park the car on the bend of a steep hill.

# Details of Trail

This walk can be enjoyed both summer and winter, but if it is attempted after periods of heavy rainfall, wellingtons or stout boots are recommended for walkers, as there can be mud and water standing in places. The walk covers a distance of 4½ miles and encompasses some beautiful woodlands, with stream and lake and, in turn, views over towards Abbeystead and Clougha Pike, Lancaster, the Lakeland hills, Morecambe Bay and the Fylde Plain.

For the nature lover many varieties of bird abound, and the woodlands contain many mature trees and smaller growth. It should be noted that the rhododendrons are spectacular in the spring. Despite its growing popularity, the walk is well maintained by the Water Authority and conservation volunteers.

The trail commences from the car-parking spot described above. Take the downhill path, which can be a little rough and requires care, to the bottom of the hill where the track joins with the main bridle path. Go through the gate and follow the stream, slightly uphill. The path goes through another gate and a view of the lake (a reservoir) is on the right. The track bears left at the end of the lake, and there is a further gate. The track then continues through rhododendron thickets to a second gate

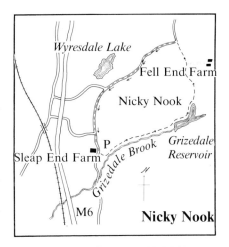

leading to a more substantial path over a small iron bridge. From here on the views previously mentioned unfold, with Grizedale Fell and its neighbours on the right, and the sprawl of Fell End Farm in the valley. The track then continues through another gate on to a metalled road which should be followed for several hundred yards. Take the first left turn and continue on this country road, with the views unfolding, noting the lake on the right and Scorton village ahead.

The going is downhill and easy, and the road should be followed bearing to the left. You will pass a cottage with a mature display of hydrangeas on the left. The road continues for approximately half a mile, passing farm buildings on the right, and returns to the start of the walk.

Whilst approximately half the trail is on metalled country roads, traffic is normally light and slow-moving except at peak holiday periods.

Facilities: Toilets are situated in Scorton village and well signposted. They are, in fact, just further on than the village bowling green (see 'Starting Point' directions above). The toilets are not identified as being for the disabled, but are reasonably 'user-friendly', with a 2-inch step and room for normal wheelchair access.

Scorton village has several shops, and there is a licensed cafe, but direct wheelchair access would be difficult without assistance.

There is easy parking in the village, though weekends and bank holiday periods are busy and should be avoided.

## Trail 38 Grade B

# Sea and Shore, Knott End

## *Starting Point*

Take the A6 from Preston, going north until the Chequered Flag public house appears on the left. You are then level with Garstang. Turn left off the A6 at the Chequered Flag and after approximately 1½ miles take the first right, signposted Knott End. Follow the Knott End signs until you reach the promenade. Parking is adjacent to the Bourne Arms, which is close by the ferry slipway, with Fleetwood across the river.

---

## Details of Trail

This is a flat walk of about three miles each way, with no gates, gradients or other difficulties. It starts with a short walk on Knott End promenade itself, where there are places to rest – as indeed there are all along the walk. The path continues from the end of the promenade along a tarmacadam walkway and follows the seashore, which is relatively unspoilt. There are views across Morecambe Bay towards the Lakeland hills. At the end of the promenade there is a diagram detailing all the names of the hills etc. which can be seen.

The walk is actually along the top of the sea defence works. Across the sea, Heysham Power Station, Glasson Dock, Lancaster University and the Williamson Memorial are in view.

The walk ends after about three miles at the slipway at Fluke Hall, which is served by a metalled road from Pilling village. The walk may be pleasantly extended down this roadway to Pilling village itself, where there are several hostelries and shops.

It is anticipated that the walk to Fluke Hall will take 1–1½ hours depending on speed and resting time, with a further half-hour (say one mile) if the trail continues to Pilling village.

Whilst the route is easy and flat, it is recommended that it be undertaken in fine weather in view of the exposed nature and lack of shelter away from the promenade proper.

Facilities: The nearest toilets are at Knott End, adjacent to the start of the walk, behind the cafe on the edge of the car park. Regrettably, they are not adapted for disabled use. The gents has a ramp to the entrance, but the ladies has three steps.

There is also a toilet block in Pilling village centre, just past the church. Again, not specifically for the disabled, but with one step up and reasonably accessible.

There are several cafes, shops etc., in Knott End itself, both on and adjacent to the promenade. The Bourne Arms public house serves bar meals, etc., and in Pilling village there are several pubs, the Golden Ball, the Ship Inn, etc., which serve food. There are also several cafes and craft shops.

# Clitheroe Town and Castle Trail

## Starting Point

Travelling on the A59 Skipton/Blackburn road from the Blackburn direction, exit left to Clitheroe. Travel right into the town centre, keeping the castle to your left. As you enter the main shopping centre you are climbing a hill. When you reach the castle gates the road bends sharply right; three hundred yards from this bend turn left, then first right. There is a car park on your right, opposite the health centre. At this point there are toilets, including ones for the disabled.

## Details of Trail

Leave the car park by the entrance you drove in at, and turn left. After about 75 yards, cross the road and take the turning next to the Norweb showrooms. This is New Market Street, and leads to the open market, which is open Tuesdays and Saturdays all year round. The road passes straight through the market and comes out on Parson Lane at the New Inn. Cross the road and turn right. Continue on this path and it will take you down past the Methodist Church, under a footbridge, and into the castle grounds.

At the entrance is the Heald Well, one of the original wells that gave Clitheroe its water supply. From this point there are two routes.

Route A: At the well turn left up a moderate gradient to the bowling greens, tennis courts and summer house. A small cafe overlooks the bowling green and operates during the summer. All these are to the right. After these diversions, take the path to the left in front of the bandstand, where open-air activity of all kinds is held.

Route B: From the well carry on past the children's play area to the open field which is the site of different events during the summer months. The path goes round the outside of the field, ending up at the bowling green etc., and you take the

path in front of the bandstand. This leads to the main castle gates, which were erected as a memorial to those killed in the Second World War. The whole of the castle grounds were bought by public subscription after the First World War as a memorial.

Turn right, still inside the castle gates. This will take you up to the museum, the cenotaph, the North West Sound Archives and the castle keep. Access to the keep is free and quite safe, but there are steps which would restrict a wheelchair or the less able. From the keep there are views of the Ribble Valley, Pendle Hill, Kemple End, and many other fells. There is also a sound system giving a commentary on the history of the keep.

Retrace your steps to the castle gate. A walk down either side of Castle Street, towards the clock in the town centre, will offer a large variety of shops, and at the Swan & Royal Hotel there is a small courtyard of shops.

Carry on to the clock in the town centre. This brings you to the market place which was the site of the old markets, including livestock, and the old political hustings.

To the left of the clock is the White Lion Hotel. Take the pedestrian way through the arch which leads to the Council Offices where the Tourist Information Office is situated, then back to the car park where you started.

Facilities: The nearest toilets suitable for wheelchairs are at the starting point of the walk, and also in the market.

Cafes: Apricot Meringue in King Street, and the Toll House, Parson Lane. Both have good entrances and helpful staff.

There are several public houses within a short distance, with single steps at the door. Toilets vary.

# Wycoller Country Park, near Colne

## Starting Point

Take the A6068 from Colne to Keighley. Turn right to Trawden on the B6250. Approaching Trawden, look for the sign to Wycoller Country Park pointing along Keighley Road. The road is on the left before the war memorial. Proceed up a steep hill (1 in 6) to the next sign for the country park on the right and follow this road to Wycoller. There is a large car park and the trail starts from here.

## Details of Trail

The footpath running parallel to the road goes downhill, joining the road to Wycoller hamlet. A stream runs through the hamlet and this must be crossed to reach the historic ruins of Wycoller Hall. The clapper bridge is just wide enough to take a wheelchair, but this needs great care and could be unnerving for the passenger. An alternative is to take the car into Wycoller to the sign for the Pendle Way at the bottom of the hill. Drive straight between two large stone gateposts, up a rough slope, past a barn on the left, and down the other side of the stream, where the passenger can get out of the car into the wheelchair. A more direct route is to drive the car across the shallow stream. Parking in Wycoller is reserved for residents and cars with a disabled sticker.

Wycoller is an historic place, often visited by the Brontes from Haworth, and a small museum gives an interesting picture of Wycoller as it was. The country walk up the Dene, of about a mile, is a steady climb. Wycoller Craft Centre offers local craft work and catering every day except Monday. The trail is only three miles, but there are many interesting cottages and country scenes. There are, however, some steep places. This walk could be combined with the Ball Grove Recreation Centre.

Facilities: The nearest toilets are

across the stream at Wycoller, behind the museum, near the lake and picnic area. Wycoller Craft Centre is the only catering establishment in the hamlet (tel: 0282 868395); it is closed on Mondays.

# Green Route and Leeds/Liverpool Canal Towpath, Burnley

## Starting Point

The trail starts outside Burnley Central Station (tel: 0282 25421), which is on Railway Street and well signed. There is ample parking outside the station. Burnley Central is on the East Lancashire Line and provides connections with Colne, Preston, Manchester and Yorkshire. Wheelchair users can use all trains on this line, and there is level access from the platform into the car park, with a disabled toilet at platform level. You will find this trail on O.S. Pathfinder Map, Burnley, sheet SD 83/93.

## Details of Trail

The total distance of the trail is eight miles, but it can be shortened to any length as required.

The Green Route is a converted disused railway with wide tarmac surface and shallow gradients, running north from the station through Thursby Gardens. If you turn left before the main path drops under the first bridge, you will be on Monk Hall Street, which has wheelchair access on to the Leeds/

Liverpool Canal towpath. Burnley Borough Council and the British Waterways Board have spent a considerable sum dramatically up-grading the towpath over the past few years, and laying a wheelchair-friendly surface, which you will use on the whole towpath section of this trail.

If you follow the disused railway you could explore Thompson Park and Bank Hall beyond, which was once the site of Bank Hall Pit. Thompson Park is a children's play park with slides and swings and safe surfaces, and a boating lake. Al-though you will not see any dogs, as they are banned, there is plenty of wildlife including grey squirrels, which have become very tame and

may take food from your hand.

When you join the canal towpath at Monk Hall Street, turn left and north towards Heald Bridge, cross the bridge and experience Barden Park, a wilderness park planted in 1989 on the site of Barden Colliery. If you follow the towpath north to the borough boundary you will have fine views of the countryside to the north, including Pendle Hill.

Retrace your steps to Monk Hall Street and continue south to the Straight Mile. Any walk in reverse will seem like a wholly new experi-ence, as the lie of the land will look quite different.

The Straight Mile embankment was built between 1796 and 1801, is sixty feet above the town, and gives the walker a fine panoramic view of the town surrounded by hills.

As you enter the Straight Mile you may be lucky enough to see young canoeists in the canoe training area. West of the Straight Mile is Finsley Gate, the other end of the trail, where you will find an interpretation panel on the towpath wall.

You could now walk back to the station via the towpath and the Green Route, or leave the towpath at Finsley Gate and walk through the town, perhaps taking in the Burnley Mechanics' Arts and Entertainment Centre on Manchester Road, with its Tourist Information Centre, disabled toilet, cafe and bar.

Facilities as mentioned in the text.

---

*Trail 42*
*Grade B*

# Langho via Painter Wood and York

## Starting Point

The trail starts from the car park at the Petre Arms, Langho, one hundred yards on the left of the A666 to Whalley, after the roundabout at the junction of the A59 to Preston and the A666 to Blackburn on the Whalley Bypass.

---

## Details of Trail

From the car park turn left towards Whalley along the A666, past St. Leonard's School. Continue along past the school to St. Augustine's at Billington. At the public house, the Judge Walmsley, look to the left over the River Calder to Whalley Abbey, founded by the monks of Stanlow Abbey in Cheshire in the thirteenth century, and occupied until its dissolution by Henry VIII in 1537.

Immediately across from the

Judge Walmsley, a road leads to Painter Wood and York. Whilst this is a little steep at the start, the gradient becomes more gradual as you round the bend. This road continues for approximately 2½ miles to York village, giving views across the Ribble Valley towards the twin towers of Stonyhurst College. Along the way a number of seats are available to rest and enjoy the view.

At the village of York, go down the road to the right to Langho, and then take the next road on the right. This will bring you to the main road at the Spring Mill Hotel. Again turn right towards the railway bridge, and after the bridge follow the path on the right down the cul-de-sac, which has a footpath to avoid the busy roundabout.

The length of the trail is 4½ miles.

Facilities: The nearest toilets suitable for wheelchairs are at the Petre Arms, Longsight Road, Langho (tel: Blackburn 0254 248169). This is also the most convenient place for refreshments and a ramp is available for entry.

# Dean Clough Reservoir Circular Walk, Great Harwood

## Starting Point

Take the A680 from Accrington towards Whalley, turning left at the signpost for Great Harwood, opposite Nightingale's garage, and travel along Harwood New Road, Harwood Lane, and Park Lane to the top of the hill by the old church. Go straight on into Cliffe Lane, and in about a quarter of a mile you will see the Dog and Otter public house on your right. The trail starts here (O.S. 103/731 331).

## Details of Trail

Turn right from the car park and follow the road uphill and round the corner into Blackburn Old Road, keeping the cricket ground on your left. In about two hundred metres, turn right down Gold-acre Lane, a steep road without a foot-path, but relatively quiet. After two hund-red metres take the public footpath signposted to your left. The track is uneven, with a cinder surface, and

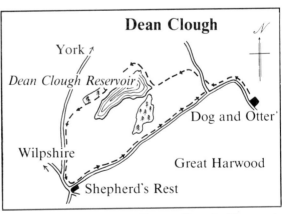

leads to Dean Clough Reservoir. Keep to the track through two gates and you will arrive at the reservoir.

(NB: all gates are unlocked and have 'kissing gate' stiles along the entire walk.)

The Dean Clough Conservation Project is taking place in this area. The Hyndburn Borough Council, with support from the North West Water Authority, is sponsoring a scheme under the Conservation Project to carry out a variety of works in the Dean Clough area to improve the facilities, such as repairs to stiles, paths, car parking etc., and to conserve wildlife and improve the natural habitat.

Turn right and pass along the north-east (broad) end of the reservoir to a gate. Through the gate the track goes uphill for about a hundred metres; this is steep, grassy, and probably one of the hardest parts of the trail. Turn left through a gate and the track now goes along the north-west (long) side of the reservoir. The track drops a little about halfway along, then climbs gently alongside a small plantation. You will pass through another gate about halfway along. The track narrows in a hundred metres, and becomes boggy for forty metres. Keep to the track for another two hundred metres and you will arrive at the York to Blackburn road. Turn left (NB: there are no pavements from this point until arriving back at

Goldacre Lane, and the roads can be busy at times) and go uphill, passing a farmhouse at the junction with Wilpshire Road. After a hundred metres, turn left at the Shepherd's Rest public house (formerly the Bay Horse New Inns). The road back towards Great Harwood is reasonably level for about a mile. On arriving at the 30mph signs there is a shelter on your left with views towards Accrington. The road now goes down a 1 in 6 hill (views towards Bowley Hill and Pendle, famous haunt of the Lancashire Witches in the early seventeenth century). At the bottom of the hill you will pass Goldacre Lane and continue around the cricket ground back to your starting point at the Dog and Otter.

Facilities: Shepherd's Rest, Wilpshire Road, Rishton, tel. (0254) 48348. There is one step at the entrance. The 'mother and baby' room is suitable for the disabled and can be used by either sex. The public house is open from 11.00am to 3.00pm and from 5.00pm to 11.00pm. Food is served from 12 noon to 2.00pm and 5.00pm to 10.00pm; The Dog and Otter, Cliffe Lane, Great Harwood, tel. (0254) 885760. There are three steps down into the bar, and the toilets will not take a wheelchair.

# Billinge Wood/Pleasington Cemetery, Blackburn

## *Starting Point*

From Blackburn town centre, take the A674 Preston and Chorley road. After two miles look for the Scapa Porritt works on the left. Opposite the works, turn right into Witton Park and park the car.

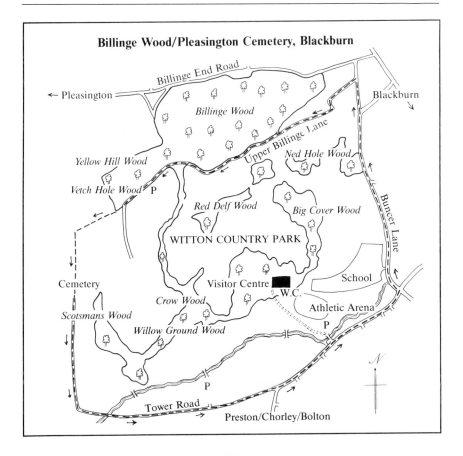

**Billinge Wood/Pleasington Cemetery, Blackburn**

## Details of Trail

The trail covers a distance of four miles.

From the car park go back to the main road and turn left towards Blackburn. At the traffic lights turn left up Buncer Lane. Go past St. Mark's Church and Witton Park Schools. At a sharp right hand bend turn left into Billinge Avenue at the end of which, turn right up the hill, then first left into Under Billinge Lane. Continue past the farm, over the cattle grid, and down through the fields to a gate. Go through the gate on to a stone path through the fields, then over the cattle grid into Pleasington Cemetery. Go past the crematorium and on down the hill into Pleasington Playing Fields. Follow the road to the top of the hill and turn left on to the main road which leads back to the start of the walk.

There are toilets and a cafe in Witton Park. The walk has good paths and no steep sections. One third of the walk is on main roads, the rest through fields, partly with woods on one side.

## Trail 45 Grade B

# Billinge Wood, Blackburn

## Starting Point

From Blackburn town centre take the A677 towards Preston. After approximately 1½ miles, turn left at the crossroads (traffic lights) towards Pleasington. Follow this road for approximately a quarter of a mile and look for an opening through the wall on the left, which leads into the car park.

## Details of Trail

From the car park turn right down the hill and follow the blue markers. At the first junction turn left down the hill (note the tree with eight trunks). Go straight on down the hill and at the next junction, when the

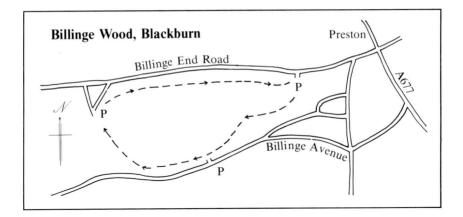

**Billinge Wood, Blackburn**

Billinge End Road

Preston

A677

Billinge Avenue

P

P

P

N

path meets the road, turn right up the hill. (If you turn left you could go back to the start via a tarmac road.)

At the cross paths go straight on up the hill – this is a very steep section.

At the car park turn right and back to the start.

There are good, defined paths but steep sections with tree roots and large stones all through the woodlands. A person in a wheelchair would need two helpers.

There are no toilets or cafe on this walk, which is a distance of two miles.

Trail 46
Grade B

# Calf Hey Trail, Haslingden

## *Starting Point*

Take the B6232 Haslingden to Blackburn road. Approximately two miles from Haslingden and about half a mile beyond the Duke of Wellington public house, take a left turn which leads to a car park.

## Details of Trail

The Calf Hey trail is a circular trail around the Calf Hey Reservoir at Haslingden Grane, and is a distance of 1½ miles.

Leave the car park through the kissing gate, bear right at the picnic area and proceed through a gate with a conifer plantation on the left.

Here are two ruined dwellings which have been excavated to reveal the ground plan. Grane village was abandoned to make way for the reservoir.

Further on you will see the remains of Hartley House Cottages on the right. At a fork in the path bear left down to another gate, then follow the path to the left. When you come to a junction, take the left hand path and continue to bear left by the side of the reservoir. As you come to

the head of the reservoir turn left across the dam. At the end of the dam take the left hand path up to a gate. Go through this and turn right, and the path leads into the car park.

Facilities: Nearest toilets: return to the main road (B6232) and turn left towards Blackburn. After about four hundred yards there is a car park on the right, and the toilets are here. There is also an information centre which is open at weekends.

The Duke of Wellington public house is on the B6232 towards Haslington (tel: 0706 215610). Here you can get Brewer's Fayre, and there are disabled toilets.

A booklet about this trail can be obtained from: Leisure Offices, 41 Kay Street, Rawtenstall, Rossendale, tel. (0706) 217777.

*Trail 47 Grade B*

# Longton Village and Brickworks

## Starting Point

Access is from the A59. Travelling west from Preston, take the second left turn at the Hutton roundabout. Pass Hutton Grammar School to the village centre, turn right at St. Andrew's Church and continue through the village, keeping to the main road. At the Golden Ball/Blundell's Corner bear left. Ignore turnings to Woodlands Way, School Lane and Drumacre Lane. The entrance to the car park is less than a hundred yards from the junction with Drumacre Lane.

If travelling east on the A59 take the second left at Hoole roundabout. Ignore the right hand fork to Walmer Bridge and continue towards the village. The entrance to the car park is on the right-hand side of the road just before the junction with Drumacre Lane.

Longton is an old village which has expanded considerably as a dormitory suburb of Preston in the past twenty or thirty years.

---

## Details of Trail

All the stiles mentioned are specially designed for use by people in wheel-chairs.

The car park is adjacent to the old brick pits, which could now better be described as lakes or meres. If only a short walk is possible, one can leave the car park from the Walmer Bridge side of the village and walk around the largest of the meres on an elevated pathway (surface Grade B), looping left to a stile on to Drumacre Lane. One can also cross Drumacre Lane by a stile. There is a two-hundred-yard walk along the side of the second mere (the third and smallest is below, on the left) to Briarcroft.

A wide range of different birds nest near the meres, and in March the following species were observed in a short space of time: mallard and tufted ducks; coots; moorhens; grebes; swans; greylag and pink-footed geese. There are seats along

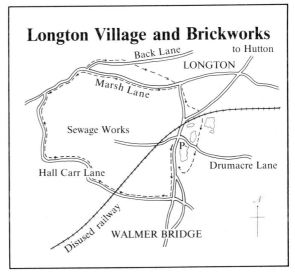

Longton Village and Brickworks

all of the walks.

Turn left through a stile into Briarcroft, left again into School Lane adjacent to Ashwood Court (a modern sheltered housing complex), and proceed to the main road. The car park is two or three hundred yards back towards Walmer Bridge, on the left hand side of the road.

For those with more time, and blessed with a fine day, there is an interesting walk of about five miles which ends with the walk round the meres described above. One should leave the car park on the mere-side path going towards Walmer Bridge. Take the stile leading to the main road. If you immediately cross the road it is possible to walk the half-mile or so to the junction with Hall Carr Lane on a footpath with a Grade A surface. Turn right onto Hall Carr Lane. There is only a sidewalk as far as the sign on the left to Hoole. There is a seat on the right a little further down the lane. One then passes between the stone retaining walls of a now-demolished bridge built for the Preston to Southport railway line, which closed in the early 1960s. One continues on the country lane for something over a mile to the junction with Marsh Lane and Hall Carr Lane. Turn right at this point, walking back towards the centre of the village of Longton.

The second lane on the left is Back Lane. One can either keep to Marsh Lane, and continue as far as the Golden Ball/Blundell's Corner, or turn left into Back Lane. Initially, the surface of Back Lane is Grade A, but after a few hundred yards it deteriorates into a green lane and a surface best rated as B-minus. The surface collects water in large puddles after heavy rain. Back Lane is almost a mile long and goes as far as the edge of the residential area. Just before this point a footpath marked on the right (still B-minus) takes one to the Golden Ball/Blundell's Corner.

When rejoining the main road from either route selected, cross the road, turn right and walk towards Walmer Bridge. Just after Woodlands Way one should go through the wrought iron gates and take a path going diagonally to the right to School Lane. There are seats in this pleasant area. Turn left into School Lane, pass Ashwood Court on your right and enter Briarcroft. Immediately on your right you will see a path leading to the brick pits. Entry is through a stile. One then walks in the reverse of the direction already described above.

Facilities: As already indicated, Longton is now a large village and there is a small shopping centre with a particularly well-regarded Booth's supermarket.

The Golden Ball has a restaurant and serves bar food. There is also the Longton Tavern which serves traditional bar food and also has a pizzeria. Access to the main building is up half a dozen steps and down a similar number to the pizzeria. Access can be made through the function room. The toilets are said to have 'wide doors'.

On the row of shops you will find Forshaw's Cafe – a good place for a cuppa and a cake. The Ram's Head is also nearby and the Anchor Hotel, situated near the Hutton round-about, is well-regarded for bar meals.

Just opposite the Ram's Head there are public conveniences. To gain access to the disabled toilet, however, one needs to purchase a key from the Environmental Health and Housing Dept., Civic Centre, West Paddock, Leyland.

The library and health centre are nearby, both with toilets for the disabled.

# The Eccleston Antique Trail

## Starting Point

Travel south on the A49 to Euxton, west of Chorley, and turn right at the Euxton Mills pub on the A581 to Euxton and Southport. After 2½ miles, and having passed the Traveller's Rest, Euxton Coach House and the Shell garage – all on the right – take a left hand turn to Eccleston, the B5250. After half a mile you cross the River Yarrow by a hump-back bridge. Park on the church car park immediately on the right, or at the Blue Anchor a little further up on the right.

## Details of Trail

Visit St. Mary's Church, quietly situated alongside the River Yarrow. Records show a church on this site as early as 1094. Across the river is Millrace, a family house converted from the village mill. Farming was

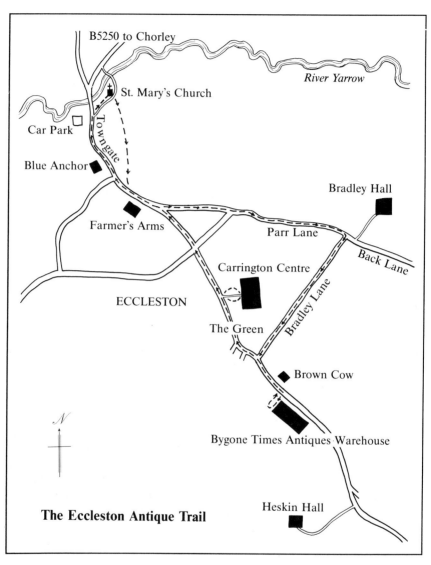

The Eccleston Antique Trail

the main livelihood of the village and there is still evidence of orchards with old-established trees, but industry developed from handloom weaving and coal mining. Only farming remains, but the mills of yesteryear now house shops, small businesses and a large antiques warehouse.

In the south-east corner of the

churchyard, away from the present entrance, is an unpaved path used by parishioners before cars were invented; this should be followed uphill. At the main road, Towngate, turn left. Several houses in the village have dates, and on the left is one dated 1659. The Farmer's Arms on the right offers up-to-date facilities behind its old exterior. Nearby is Bank House, now a private house but originally the village bank, founded in 1818 and amalgamated with the TSB in 1919. Next door is the old school, built in 1834 and in need of renovation. You are now ten miles from Preston on what used to be the Penwortham–Wrightington turnpike. Turn left into Parr Lane, which has a variety of interesting old houses and cottages. After half a mile and at the junction with Bradley Lane, look north-east: there are open country views with farm buildings, and the nearby manor house of Bradley Hall tucked away in the trees.

Proceed up Bradley Lane past the local football and playing fields. At the junction with the main road, now The Green, turn left. Just past the Brown Cow is Bygone Times, an antique and architectural warehouse.

The building used to be Grove spinning and weaving mill, employing three hundred people in 1861, and backing on to Sydbrook. Grove Crescent was built to house some of its employees.

Two of the three floors are easily accessible by wheelchairs and the goods on offer are guaranteed to capture your interest: the variety is enormous. The toilets are usually accessible. The cafe is entered by means of a short stair (five steps) and a walk through the third floor and has further toilet facilities. None of the toilet facilities is specially suited for wheelchair users.

After leaving Bygone Times, retrace your steps along The Green. Do not turn into Bradley Lane, but continue through the village. The Carrington Centre on the right is also a converted mill. It includes a library which has a copy of *Eccleston and Heskin in Times Past*, produced by the local Historical Society, and from which several references have been taken in the above text. There is also a cafe (with ramp access) for refreshments and a break, before returning to The Green and proceeding back to your parked car.

Facilities as mentioned in the text.

# Astley Park Trail, Chorley

## Starting Point

Travel south on the A6 to Chorley town centre. At the town hall (on the right) turn right for Southport on the A581. Parking is available by turning right at the rear of the police headquarters and town hall, and directly ahead across Queen's Road.

## Details of Trail

Turn right from the car park, and the start of this 2½-mile trail is along a suburban street. At the junction with Southport Road turn right and proceed down the hill. If you care to watch a game of cricket, the Chorley Cricket Club is signposted just off to the left along Southport Road. At the bottom of the hill, after passing the school playing fields and just before the black-and-white timbered house, is an entrance on the right over a bridge to Astley Park. The road winds through the woods with the River Chor alongside, then up a substantial rise to the bowling greens. The gardens and greens can be enjoyed while taking a well-earned respite. It is then a short walk to Astley Hall, which is open between 12.00 and 5.30pm from April to September, and a tearoom open from 10.30am to 4.00pm. Disabled toilets are available from 2.00pm.

Astley Hall is one of the oldest buildings in Chorley, with an impressive range of windows on the front. In the late-seventeenth century these were added to the oldest part of the house, built in the sixteenth century. The entrance opens into the Great Hall with its superb double-storey bay window, an impressive plaster ceiling and many wood panel portraits. It contains the famous Sirloin Chair, used by James I when he knighted a loin of beef at Hoghton Tower. The Morning Room has the second grand bay window, timber panelling and plaster ceiling, while the Drawing Room ceiling is even more ornate than that in the Great Hall. The kitchens are a reminder of days gone by. Although the other floors are open to visitors there is no lift, but the guide book has a good set of pictures and text, particularly relat-

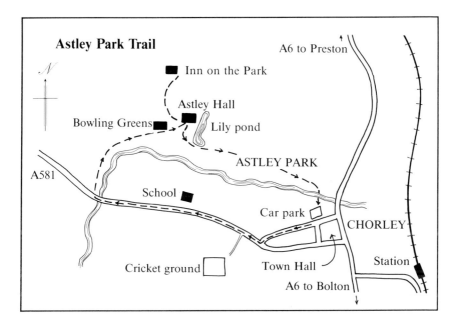

**Astley Park Trail**

A6 to Preston

Inn on the Park

Astley Hall

Bowling Greens

Lily pond

ASTLEY PARK

A581

School

Car park

CHORLEY

Cricket ground

Town Hall

Station

A6 to Bolton

ing to the 'shovel board' in the Long Gallery on the top floor. Elsewhere there is a World War Remembrance Room, and the collection of Leeds pottery and antique glass.

At the side of the hall is a superb lilly pond generally adorned with swans and ducks. The path passes over the end of the pond and up to the small animal park with rabbits, sheep, ducks etc., for children to admire. The park is home to the Royal Lancashire Show at the end of July each year; a charge is made for admission to the grounds then, so avoid the park on Show weekend. The park is spacious and amply wooded with plenty of room for your dog to run, or for you to enjoy a picnic. There is a children's play area and a paddling pool. The main exit is directly ahead through the large memorial arch gate, but the path bearing right returns you to the car park.

Facilities as mentioned in the text.

# Entwistle Reservoir Trail

## Starting Point

Take the A666 from Darwen towards Bolton. Turn left on to the B6391 (Greens Arms Road), and take a left turn down Bartridge Road to a car park by the reservoir.

## Details of Trail

The trail is a 2½-mile (4km) circular walk round the reservoir. At the time of writing there was easy access for wheelchairs from the car park turning left to the end of the reservoir.

Turning right from the car park there is wheelchair access round the reservoir as far as Simms Meadow, but at present the footpaths between Simms Meadow and the end of the reservoir are difficult and less suitable for wheelchairs. It is hoped that this may be remedied in the future.

Facilities: A toilet block is to be built on the car park, and possibly a cafe and information centre.

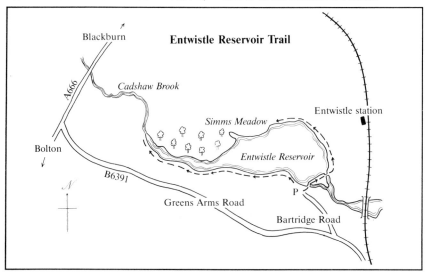

Entwistle Reservoir Trail

Blackburn

Cadshaw Brook

A666

Simms Meadow

Entwistle station

Bolton

Entwistle Reservoir

B6391

Greens Arms Road

P

Bartridge Road

N

# Uldale Chapel House Reservoir and Overwater

## Starting Point

Take the A591 from Keswick to Carlisle. After approximately seven miles turn right for Uldale at the Castle Inn. Over the crossroads in the village is the Snooty Fox Inn, which is the starting point for the trail.

## Details of Trail

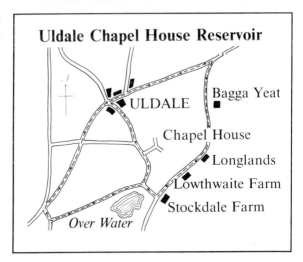

**Uldale Chapel House Reservoir**

ULDALE
Bagga Yeat
Chapel House
Longlands
Lowthwaite Farm
Stockdale Farm
*Over Water*

This is a circular trek of approximately eight miles in a hilly area, with some steep inclines. It may be advisable to have more than one pusher per wheelchair.

Turn left from the T-junction up the hill towards Caldbeck. It is a long and steep incline, but rewarding. On the first corner over the cattle grid the Solway coast comes into view. Travel for a further half-mile and turn right at the sign for Orthwaite 2½ miles and Mirkholme 3½ miles. Brae Fell is on your left and Longlands, foothills to Skiddaw, one of England's highest mountains, is straight ahead. Half a mile along the fell road comes a cattle grid, and the sheep farm on the left is Baggra Yeat. Another half-mile along the road is the hamlet of Longlands. To the right is the first glimpse of

Overwater Lake. Pass Lowthwaite Farm and down the hill on the right you will see Chapel House Reservoir. Travel to Stockdale Farm and turn right towards Uldale. The lake is on the left. Go over the bridge and the gate on the left takes you to the lakeside. The road then forks up a steep hill towards Uldale, or you can travel alongside the lake, turning right at the junction, and then right again for Uldale, which is a further three miles but which gives you a magnificent view of Bassenthwaite Lake.

The hill from Overwater Lake to Uldale is steep, but that route is five miles. Travelling round the lakeside, the distance is eight miles.

Facilities: There are disabled toilets with helpful staff at the Snooty Fox Inn, Uldale (tel: 0965 7479), which also serves good meals.

# Dash Falls, Keswick

## Starting Point

Take the A591 from Keswick to Carlisle. After approximately six miles turn
right at Bassenthwaite Chapel. Half a mile along the road is Bassenthwaite
village, and the trail starts at the Sun Inn.

## Details of Trail

The trek is approxi-
mately six miles by
road, but the Dash
Falls trail from the
road should only be
encountered by those
prepared with two
pushers per chair. The
proper outdoor cloth-
ing for the climate and
terrain should also be
carried.

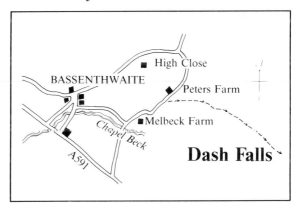

■ High Close

BASSENTHWAITE

◆ Peters Farm

■ Melbeck Farm

Chapel Beck

A591

**Dash Falls**

Turn right from the
Sun Inn car park, along a treed
avenue. Turn left at the next junction and then immediately left off
the main road, heading along a single
track road into the folds of Skiddaw
(one of England's highest mountains). Beware of on-coming traffic. It
is half a mile to Burthwaite Farm.
The road is criss-crossed with public
footpaths, and you are likely to meet
hikers on the way.

The road steepens through a
beautiful wooded canopy alongside
Chapel Beck for a mile. Turn left at

the junction marked 'Uldale 4, Caldbeck 8½'. Travel up the hill past
Melbeck's Farm on the right.

At the top of the hill, just before
Peter's House at the start of the fir
trees, you will see a sign on the right
for a public bridleway leading to
Skiddaw House and Threlkeld via
Dash Falls. It is a good tarmac road
all the way along, but make sure to
close the gates behind you to keep
the sheep in.

The white crag on your left is
Brockle Crag, nesting-place of

ravens, carrion crows and jackdaws. One mile further up, on the right, is the track road leading to Dash Falls.

The path is accessible by wheelchair and climbs alongside the falls up to fifteen hundred feet. Skiddaw House is a hostel some two miles further along the track, but I do not recommend you to venture this far.

The turn-back point would be the base of the falls. Remember that at this altitude, and according to the time of the year, the weather can change adversely, so do not push on further than comfort and conditions dictate.

On return to the road, turn right past Peter House Farm, which is on the main road. This will bring you to a bridge just past Mirk Holme sheep farm. Turn left to Bassenthwaite and follow the Dash Beck back into Bassenthwaite for 1½ miles. This road leads you through the Forestry Commission land of Park Wood. It is all downhill back into Bassenthwaite, with Kestrel Lodge and High Close on the left. Round the corner, and just over the old stone bridge into Bassenthwaite, is the Sun Inn.

Facilities: The Sun Inn, Bassenthwaite, tel. 059-681-439. The toilets are not very suitable for wheelchairs, but the staff are helpful; The Calvert Trust toilets, back on the A591 towards Keswick, may be used until 4.30pm daily; The Snooty Fox Inn, Uldale, has custom-built toilets for the disabled. The staff are helpful and the food good.

# Foot of Cat Bells and Manesty Woods

## Starting Point

Leave the M6 at junction 40 (Keswick–Penrith) and take the A66 to Keswick. Keep on the A66 past Keswick (or if in Keswick, take the B5289 out of Keswick) on the road to Cockermouth and Workington. Soon after the last sign to Keswick, turn left at the sign for Portinscale, Lingholm Gardens and Grange. Travel through the village of Portinscale and follow the road round, always following the signs for Grange. Keep on past Lingholm Gardens on your left until, nearly two miles from Portinscale, the road begins to climb on a Z-bend. Cross the cattle grid and, at the next bend, go straight ahead following the sign for the car park.

## Details of Trail

This walk (total length approximately four miles) will require two helpers (for a light passenger) or three helpers to negotiate the more difficult parts. The first part is hilly and has some rough terain. The return trip is on narrow roads and requires caution.

Leave the car park and walk back to the bend in the road. Ignore all footpath signs, as these paths are unsuitable for wheelchairs. From the bend proceed up the road a short distance (care needed) until a gravel path appears on your right with a steep slope. Do not follow the sign

for the Cat Bells Bridge footpath; instead, take the track up the hill. At the top of this rise you will be on the main path and will have a magnificent view of Derwentwater and the surrounding hills which will remain with you for much of the walk, so stop frequently to admire the view.

The path is generally level and quite smooth, but helpers are necessary as parts of the path have fallen away in places. At the end of the path, when it joins the road again, there is also a fairly large drop. This can be negotiated with helpers – and with care – and the walk completed back down the road to the car park. Alternatively, you can retrace your steps on the hillside. High up to your right will be Cat Bells, and, below you, Manesty Woods. Make sure that it is a clear day; the views are wonderful.

Facilities: The nearest toilets suitable for wheelchair users are at the Derwentwater Hotel, Portinscale, though they are not ideal. The best disabled toilets are in the central car park in Keswick. National key system, or borrow key from the Information Centre, Moot Hall, Keswick. Bar or restaurant food is available at the Derwentwater Hotel (tel: Keswick 72538) and the staff are helpful. There are numerous other pubs and cafes in Keswick town centre, many with level entrances, but not with ideal toilets.

**Trail 54
Grade C**

# Scales Farm Inn to Mill Inn, Mungrisedale

## Starting Point

Take the A66 trunk road to Penrith from Threlkeld. The Scales Farm Inn (The White Horse) is about 1½ miles on the left (GR 344269).

## Details of Trail

The trail is a distance of eight miles return, following an unadopted tarmac road to Mungrisedale (GR 365 301). There is a steep pull up to Comb Beck, and an even steeper pull after this, but this provides a pleasant four-mile (6km) route in each direction.

Facilities: The walk starts at the White Horse Inn, Scales and finishes at the Mill Inn, Mungrisedale. Refreshments and toilets are available at both of these places.

# The unspoiled Ennerdale Valley

## *Starting Point*

Leave the M6 motorway at junction 40 (Penrith) and take the A66 towards Keswick and Cockermouth to the Cockermouth junction of the A5086, which is signposted for Egremont. Follow this road for about seven miles and look for the Pack of Hounds public house on the right. Carry on for about half a mile and take a left hand turn signposted to Kirkland. On entering Kirkland village, turn left at the crossroads towards Croasdale. After ¾ mile turn left into the hamlet of Croasdale and continue on the road to Bowness Knott car park, alongside Ennerdale Lake. This is the starting point of the trail.

## *Details of Trail*

The trail covers a maximum distance of twelve miles, but this can be shortened to suit the walker.

The trail starts at the Bowness Knott car park and progresses into the upper reaches of the Ennerdale Valley along a metalled forestry access road. This is not a public road, and traffic is minimal (Forestry Commission and local residents only). For about the first 1½ miles the trail runs alongside Ennerdale Lake, and picnic facilities are available in this area. The road continues up the Ennerdale Valley for about another 4½ miles, terminating at a second youth hostel at the end of the valley. It should be noted that there is a gradual climb, particularly at the far end of the valley, which will require consideration.

The return journey is via the same route, so the total distance travelled is left to the discretion of the individual.

Points of Interest: Ennerdale is the most westerly of all the lakes in the Lake District and, because of its isolation, has not become over-run with tourists. It is an ideal setting to enjoy peace and tranquility away from the 'madding crowd'. Points of interest are the Forestry Commission plantations, where felling and replanting are regular features. In addition, the unspoiled nature of the Ennerdale Valley exhibits spectacular mountain views on both sides of the route. Special attention is drawn to the famous Pillar Rock, which is well known to rock climbers.

A special point of interest to the ornithologist is the possibility of seeing various species of wild fowl, particularly at the eastern end of the lake, and in the Bowness Knott area you may be lucky and see peregrine falcons. If not, then you will most certainly see hawks and buzzards seeking their prey.

Facilities: There are toilets suitable for wheelchairs at Bowness Knott. These are open from Easter to 31st October. There are also toilets at Low Gillerthwaite Field Centre which are wide enough to take wheelchairs. You can picnic at Bowness Knott, but there are no refreshment facilities on the trail. The nearest are: The Fox and Hounds, Ennerdale Bridge, Ennerdale Village, tel. Lamplugh (0946) 861373. Good access and ordinary toilets. This inn is approximately two miles from Bowness Knott; The Pack of Hounds, Lamplugh, tel. Lamplugh (0946) 861232. Good access and ordinary toilets. You will have passed this inn on the way to the start of the trail.

**Trail 56
Grade C**

# Hodbarrow Nature Reserve Trail

## Starting Point

Millom is a small town on the Cumbrian coast, on the west side of the Duddon Estuary.

Enter on the A5093 from the A595. Turn left over the railway bridge, following the sign for the town centre, and immediately left again at the 'free car park' sign. The car park is on the left. (Vehicles more than seven feet high must continue for a hundred yards, and use the lorry park, or Safeway's car park.)

# Details of Trail

This route is about four miles. It is nearly level, and the going is rough but described as 'bumpy' rather than 'bone-shaking' by our route-maker, who propelled himself the whole way without help in 2½ hours. He recommends that you allow four or five hours to enjoy the trip, the birds and the spectacular scenery of Black Combe, White Combe, Coniston Fells and Furness Fells.

This can be a circular tour, returning to the car park in Millom, or you can send your transport on to meet you in Haverigg, where there is a car park across the road from the Harbor Hotel.

The route goes through the town to the Hodbarrow Hollow, which is flooded mining subsidence retained

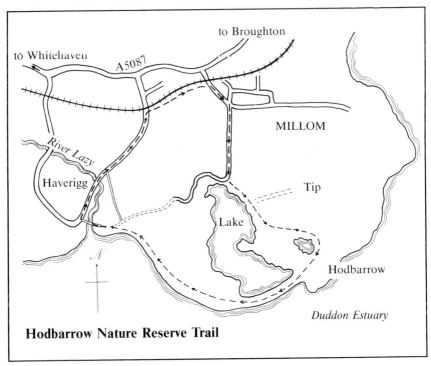

**Hodbarrow Nature Reserve Trail**

by a sea wall which kept the sea out of the mine. (For more information, read *Cumberland Iron* by A. Harris, published by D.B. Barton in 1970.) The area is an RSPB Reserve, and in summer the west end is a water-sports centre. (Members contact RSPB for information, tel: (0767) 80551.) There is a very large population of winter migrant birds and in the summer, swans, ducks, grebes and terns breed here.

Leave the car park and cross directly to the West County Hotel. Turn right, go to the corner, and cross to the church gate. Turn left past three banks (Barclays is accessible to wheelchairs) and the post office, past the Folk Museum and the Tourist Information Centre (open in summer, mining exhbition, wheelchair-usable). On the other side of the road go past the park, cross Lowther Road and turn right into Mainsgate Road. After about 1½ miles turn left at the water's edge along the track. Ignore both the left turn to the tip after 120 yards, and the right fork along the water's edge to the RSPB fence after 300 yards; instead, after 700 yards, take the right fork round Daylight Mine Pond to Hodbarrow.

To your left, see the old windmill, to which you can gain access from the grass slope on the north side, with the assistance of two strong helpers. To your right is the original stone lighthouse (no access) and, in the distance, the later, iron light-house. Go to this, looking out to the left to the estuary and Barrow-in-Furness, and to the right to the Hollow and the fells beyond. Go on along the sea wall to the caravan site and turn left along the road. (Do not turn right, unless you want to take a short cut back to the starting point.) Cross the bridge into the old village of Haverigg.

Leave Haverigg with the River Lazy on your right. From the bridge there is a sidewalk. Just before the railway bridge, turn right along the railway-side footpath and return to the start.

Facilities: Toilets for the disabled at the starting point, and in Haverigg. A radar key can be obtained from the Council Office (tel: 772666) during office hours, or buy one from L. Brownrigg, St. Bees (0946) 822585); from your local association for the disabled; or from Radar, 25 Mortimer Street, London W1N 8AB (tel: 071-637-5400).

Children's playgrounds in Millom Park and on Haverigg foreshore, two hundred yards past the toilets.

Meals can be obtained at: West County Hotel, Millom, tel. (0229) 772227. Access OK, but toilets not for wheelchair users; Harbor Hotel, Haverigg, tel. (0229) 772764. Poor access. Seats outside; Rising Sun Hotel, Haverigg, tel. (0229) 774752. Car park. Access to the dining area is easy, but the toilets are not adapted for wheelchair users.

# Worsthorne Moor, near Burnley

## Starting Point

Hurstwood is 5kms east of Burnley town centre. From the football ground, follow Brunshaw Road and Brownside Road to Worsthorne, leaving the village heading south to Hurstwood Lane, which is signed for Hurstwood. Follow the road through the village and turn right over a bridge onto an unsurfaced track just before the telephone kiosk. Hurstwood Common has extensive parking facilities and a number of picnic tables. You will find this trail on O.S. Pathfinder maps Burnley, sheet SD83/93, and Rawtenstall and Hebden Bridge, sheet SD 82/92.

## Details of Trail

This trail offers two options for the fit wheelchair user: either a circular route from Hurstwood to Cant Clough Reservoir, or a linear route from Hurstwood via Sheddon Clough to the Long Causeway. Both routes would need able-bodied helpers; two per chair for the circular route and at least three per chair for the linear route.

If you complete the circular walk with its detours, you will have covered five kilometres; if you are intrepid and tackle the linear route, you will have completed eight kilometres. Allow a full day for the linear route, and half a day for the circular

trail. Be sure to go equipped for moorland conditions; that is, maps, walking boots, and warm and waterproof clothing.

The tarmac track rising through the coniferous woodland to Hurstwood Reservoir is the start for both routes. Once at Hurstwood Reservoir, there are two short diversions. There is a walk along the dam which gives an exhilarating sense of elevation, but the kissing gate would need careful negotiation. You could be helped through by your companions while your collapsed wheelchair is passed over the top. The track on the eastern edge of the reservoir has

a good, level stone surface.

Back on the main route, there is a short, sharp climb before the stone track levels off and then drops sharply, finishing with a steep concrete section to Cant Clough Reservoir. Another detour here along the northern shore of the reservoir. Turn right through the kissing gate for the smooth tarmac track leading down to Hurstwood Common to complete the circular trail. There are two kissing gates in this section.

Walk south along the Cant Clough Reservoir dam to continue the linear trail. A short climb here on a good stone surface, but as the path levels off it becomes wet and muddy.

Here your able-bodied companions will start to 'earn their keep'! Turn left and south over the packhorse bridge. You are now in Sheddon Clough, where you will see the remains of opencast mining for lime during the seventeenth and eighteenth centuries. If you wish to discover more about these limestone hushings, you can obtain a leaflet, *A Guide to Sheddon Clough*, from Tourist Information Centres.

The next obstacle is a ford, where everyone will need good walking boots or wellingtons, and your group will have to work out the best way to cross. The next four hundred metres you may find very difficult: you will encounter large stones, mud, uneven surfaces, loose gravel, and water. After this conditions improve, with a specially prepared surface rising to the Long Causeway, and a wheelchair-size kissing gate leading to the car park.

Facilities: It is hoped that North West Water will convert the Hurstwood Pumping Station into a 'Water Collection' museum, with disabled toilets and a cafe.

The future: Burnley Borough Council are keen to improve their countryside wheelchair access, so if you have any suggestions for improving Burnley's trails, please contact the Rights of Way Officer at the Council Offices.

Trail 58
Grade C

# The Dog and Otter to York Village

## Starting Point

Take the A6064 (Harwood Road) from Rishton to Great Harwood, pass through the town and turn left along Cliffe Lane by St. Bartholomew's Church. Follow Cliffe Lane for approximately one mile to the Dog and Otter public house.

## Details of Trail

The total length of the trail is metalled.

Begin the trail at the Dog and Otter, cross the road and follow the footpath around the cricket field on to Blackburn Old Road. After approximately a third of a mile, turn right off Blackburn Old Road into Goldacre Lane, which leads into Showcliffe Lane. Follow the road down the hill for ⅔ mile to Sunny Bank. Facing you is Miles Hill. Follow the road past Allsprings House and, just after passing this

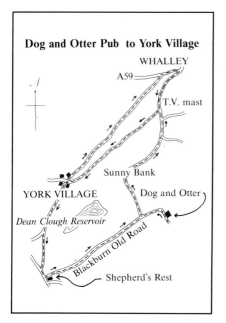

**Dog and Otter Pub to York Village**

WHALLEY

A59

T.V. mast

Sunny Bank

YORK VILLAGE

Dog and Otter

Dean Clough Reservoir

Blackburn Old Road

Shepherd's Rest

point, you can observe the bottom of the valley you have crossed. Take the next left onto Moor Lane, follow the road up the rise and pass through a farm with the farmhouse on the right and the farm buildings on the left.

Continue on past Miles Hill Farm, which is on the left. At this point you are 2½ miles from the start of the trail. Follow the road past a small pine plantation on the left, and continue on to York village, which is approximately a mile away.

From York village you have a choice of three return journeys:

1. Retrace your steps, returning the way you came. Total distance: seven miles.

2. Go through the village, taking the road to Blackburn. After about a mile the road forks. Take the left fork, keeping on the same road until you reach the Shepherd's Rest public house (formerly the Bay Horse New Inns). Take the left turn before the public house and con-tinue down to Great Harwood and the Dog and Otter. Total distance: 6½ miles.

3. With the village behind you, continue down the road towards Whalley. At a hairpin bend the road meets the A59 Preston to Skipton road. Turn right down to Whalley, but do not cross the bridge over the River Calder. Instead, turn right up a fairly steep macadam road. After nearly a mile this road forks. Take the left fork. You have now gone a full circle and can retrace your steps back to the Dog and Otter. Total distance: eight miles.

Facilities: The Game Cock, Cockbridge, Great Harwood, tel. (0254) 883719. Has toilets for the disabled. Good food; The Dog and Otter, Cliffe Lane, Great Harwood, tel. (0254) 885760. Three steps down into bar. Toilets will not take wheelchairs.

# Bowley Hill Adventure Trail, Great Harwood

## Starting Point

Ordnance Survey sheet 103, ref. 731331.

From the A680 Accrington to Whalley road, take the A6064 into Great Harwood at Nightingale's garage, by the golf club. Within ¾ mile, where the road turns sharp left downhill by the church, go forward into Cliffe Lane. The trail begins at the Dog and Otter public house, about five hundred yards on the right. There is a large car park at the rear.

From Rishton, take the A6064 to Great Harwood. Go straight ahead, uphill, at the roundabouts by the town hall clock, turning left into Cliffe Lane at the top of the hill, where the road swings sharp right at the church.

## Details of Trail

A trail of lovely views, 2½ miles one way, taking about two hours. Two able-bodied helpers are needed to negotiate a wheelchair over a difficult two-hundred-yard stretch, which is fully described.

If travelling one way, transport will have to be arranged accordingly. A return route is described, but is hillier.

One hundred and fifty yards from the Dog and Otter, take the road signed towards Bowley Scout Camp. As the road levels and then drops, note Bowley Hill on the left and, in front, the lovely panorama with Pendle Hill prominent.

With half a mile, note the sign 'Bee Breeding Station', and then on the left Hawthorne Cottage, dated 1805. Cotton weaving was done here before any factories were built.

Note the elaborate gateway to Bowley Camp. Follow the blue public footpath sign to the left, but look round Bowley first, where you will be welcome. This is East Lancashire's main scout camping site and training facility, with a full-time warden. Return to the blue footpath sign.

The next two hundred yards are

— 101 —

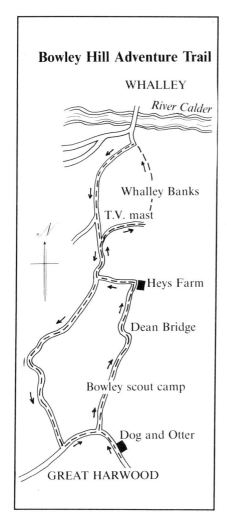

## Bowley Hill Adventure Trail

WHALLEY

*River Calder*

Whalley Banks

T.V. mast

Heys Farm

Dean Bridge

Bowley scout camp

Dog and Otter

GREAT HARWOOD

Berry's Lane, which you follow by keeping left up the hill.

On the left, note the good view of Bowley Camp and, higher up, Bowley Hill which looks much more impressive from here.

Turn right at the top by Moor End bungalow. There are good views on the right prior to a sharp left bend. Ninety yards after the bend, look for the gritstone outcropping on the right, where a perfect millstone lies among the rocks, clearly made there for the flour mill in Whalley but never needed. Here you can turn around to admire Bowley Hill and the deep valley below it.

Take the right turn (marked 'unsuitable for heavy goods vehicles') at the next junction. Note the large TV mast in front, serving Whalley. Follow the tarmac road, swinging to the right and downhill. The road goes between The Croft and White Goat Farm then, swinging left (and marked 'Dean Lane, Whalley Banks'), passes through a small former-farming community and soon becomes a cinder track.

Unhook the chain across the track, which marks the start of a private motor road. Note the attractive landscaped section on the left past the last house.

The route swings left over a cattle grid with a terraced track overlooking Whalley village. Stop by the seat and enjoy the view. Proceed over another cattle grid, turn right down a steep hill (1 in 4) to Whalley

tricky: a neglected track, deeply rutted, and with the remains of cobbles. It drops to Dean Bridge, a very pretty spot. Up the far side, negotiate seven log steps, where the chair will need to be manhandled.

Proceed over a softish track to Heys Farm to join a tarmac road,

Bridge.

Go over the bridge into Whalley, noting the flour mill on the left and the mill stream under the road, made by the monks of Whalley Abbey. Try to see the ancient church, and the ruins of the abbey closed by Henry VIII.

For a pleasant return, retrace your steps to the steep hill but keep on up it, always going straight forward. This leads back to Great Harwood, and at the T-junction on the last hill, turn left and follow the road down to the Dog and Otter.

Facilities: The nearest toilets suitable for wheelchair users are the public toilets in Whalley (behind the health centre in King Street), and at the Swan Hotel, 62 King Street, Whalley.

The nearest hotels/cafes/public houses accessible by wheelchair: All four Whalley pubs/hotels welcome wheelchairs. Cafes are not a good bet due to lack of space. The best is the Tudor Rose, 73 King Street (tel: 0254 822462) opposite the bus station, which can accommodate wheelchairs, though not with ease. Toilets there are more accessible for ladies than for men, but are not very suitable.

Current first choice of pubs: Swan Hotel, 62 King Street, Whalley, tel. (0254) 822195; Whalley Arms, King Street, Whalley, tel. (0254) 822800. Open all day Monday to Saturday from 12.00pm. Closed Sunday between 3.00pm and 6.00pm. Quite big, food is served, access direct from main car park. Toilets small for ladies, better for men. Staff helpful; Dog Inn, 55 King Street, Whalley, tel. (0254) 823009. Smaller pub. Food is served, access is easy. Toilets small for ladies, better for men. Very understanding landlord.

# The Rise to the Golf Ball, Burnley

## Starting Point

Take the A682 from Rawtenstall to Burnley, along Burnley Road through Crawshawbooth, Loveclough and Dunnockshaw. After approximately five miles you will seen the Waggoners public house on the left. Pull into the car park, and the trail starts from here.

## Details of Trail

Leave the Waggoners car park and walk on the A682 as if going back to Rawtenstall. You will notice the Clowbridge Reservoir on the left. Walk for about a mile until you see the old school house (named 'Sedge Moor') at Dunnockshaw. Take an immediate right just past the house. The road rises to a cattle grid (with a gate), keeps rising for about 250 yards and then levels off by two houses. It then rises gently for about half a mile (beware of sheep). After half a mile there is an open gate which leads to the 'Golf Ball'; this part of the road is very steep, so rests may be needed. At the top the views are breathtaking.

Return by the same route. Overall the distance is four miles.

Facilities: The nearest toilets, and the nearest refreshments, are at the Waggoners, Manchester Road, Burnley (tel: 0282 21705). No steps at the entrance. Two doors at the entrance. Entrance to toilet small, and no facilities for wheelchairs.

# Haslam Park and Lancaster Canal, Preston

## Starting Point

Travelling along the Blackpool road in the direction of Blackpool, from the eastern side of Preston, the park is situated on the right between Woodplumpton Road and the railway bridge. There is a car park.

## Details of Trail

The path leads through the park, past a pool and Bostock's Farm, down to the Lancaster Canal. Turn left on to the canal bank and continue into the country.

This walk can continue for several miles, but remember you have to make the return journey to the car park!

Facilities: Toilets at the park gates, but none for wheelchairs at the time of going to print. Preston Council hope to have toilets suitable for the disabled built soon.

Parkside Cafe opposite the park entrance, and cafes and public houses at the corner of Woodplumpton Road.

# Further Places of Interest

## Bacup

Stubbylee Park is suitable for wheelchairs. The park contains tennis courts, bowling greens, rose gardens, aviary and small animals pens. Parking is near Stubbylee Hall, now the offices of the Rossendale Council Planning and Engineering Departments.

## Bamber Bridge

The Cuerden Valley Park Trail starts at the Town Brow car park located on Lancaster Lane, the B5266, which links the A49 and the A6 approximately two miles south of Bamber Bridge. The trail is about 1½ miles long. Map and details from Lancashire Development Corporation, Cuerden Hall, Bamber Bridge, Preston PR5 6AX.

## Barrow-in-Furness

Barrow-in-Furness Borough Council has produced a booklet of heritage trails which contains:

1. The Barrow-in-Furness Urban Trail.
2. Biggar Village Trail.
3. Furness Abbey.
4. Vickerstown Trail.
5. The Dalton-in-Furness Heritage Trail.
6. Lindal-in-Furness Trail.

The booklet can be obtained from the Director of Development, Town Hall, Barrow-in-Furness, Cumbria, LA14 2LD (tel: 0229 25500).

# Bassenthwaite Lake

Map reference 234 282. Wheelchair walk with guide wire for the blind and visually handicapped.

# Blackpool

Blackpool Zoo is accessible to wheelchairs and cafes and toilets are available. Stanley Park is a large area suitable for wheelchairs. There are toilets for the disabled, and the cafe is open every day from Easter to the end of the illuminations. The promenade is several miles of flat surface along the seafront.

# Bowness-on-Windermere

A leaflet on Bowness-on-Windermere can be obtained from the Tourist Information Centre, Victoria Street, Windermere, LA23 1AD (tel: 09662 6499) The leaflet includes a street map, with toilets and parking facilities clearly shown, and suggested walks include:

1. From Rayrigg Road through the fields by Low Miller Ground, down the lakeside and back to the road through Rayrigg Meadow.
2. Cross the ferry. A walk along the lakeside to Waterloo Gardens, and possibly beyond.
3. From Glebe Road along the lakeside to the ferry.
4. From Church Street, a circular walk via Elleray Wood.

# Brockhole

Brockhole is the National Park Visitor Centre. It is on the A591 between Windermere and Ambleside. There is an admission fee. Facilities include toilets, cafes, exhibitions, film centre, craft centre. There are extensive grounds down to the lake.

# Derwentwater

Surprise View, Watendlath Road, Derwentwater (map ref. 269195). National Trust car park and viewpoint.

# Ennerdale.

Map ref. 109155. Car park. Pleasant walk suitable for wheelchairs on lake shore forestry road.

# Keswick

Keswick Railway Footpath. There is a four-mile, mainly level, footpath which follows part of the Cockermouth, Keswick and Penrith railway line along the River Greta, providing a peaceful and attractive valley route. The section from GR 299247, the junction of the Glenderaterra with the River Greta, to Low Briery Holiday Village (GR 286242) is suitable for wheelchairs.

Hope Park provides pleasant walks with access points at either end.

Lingholm Gardens, park outside the main house. Toilets accessible for wheelchairs in outbuilding. Tearoom accessible via ramp at the rear. Most of the garden and woodland are accessible.

# Lytham St. Annes

It is possible for a person in a wheelchair to go from Lytham right through to the northern end of St. Annes, with views of the estuary and sea, and with access to a variety of cafes, car parks and toilets adapted for the disabled.

Suitable toilets include:

1. Adjacent to the Lowther Gardens pavilion at Lytham. There is also a cafe with ramped access.
2. The east end of Fairhaven Lake with ramped access, and about two hundred metres from a cafe.

3. On the south-east side of St. Annes pier, with ramped access. Parking is restricted, but there is a pay and display car park in front of the pier.
4. In the new St. Annes railway station on the south-west side of the railway line.
5. In the Ansdell Institute building on Woodland Road, Ansdell.

Both St. Annes and Lytham have a 'town trail', copies of which can be obtained from the County Information Centre, 4 Clifton Square, St. Annes, or at both the Lytham and the St. Annes libraries.

# North West Water

In this book there are several trails planned by North West Water. Other trails are:
— Jumbles Reservoir Trail – a circular trail on roads, round the reservoir with a route to Turton Tower. Distance 2¾ miles (4.5km). The car park is reached from the A676 Bradshaw Road. There is an information centre and toilets for the handicapped in the car park. Information cards for all the North West Water Trails in the area may be obtained at the information centre. There are fishing facilities for the disabled at Jumbles Reservoir. Anglers need an NRA rod licence only.
— Worthington Lake – leave the M6 at junction 27 for Standish, go through the traffic lights to the A5106 and turn left. Worthington Lake is on the right. There is a trail round both rservoirs, toilets for the disabled, an information centre and countryside classroom.
— Upper Rivington Reservoir – there is an information centre at Great House Barn, Rivington and a trail, suitable for wheelchairs, right round Upper Rivington Reservoir.
— Anderton Hall Sailing Centre is situated on Lower Rivington Reservoir. This sailing centre specialises in sailing for handicapped people. For further information telephone 'First Rivington' (formerly Greater Manchester Youth Association) 0257 483304.

# Preston

Avenham/Miller Park: From Preston town centre, go down Fishergate to the traffic lights near the Midland Bank. Turn left and go straight on to the park entrance. There is street parking nearby. This park is one of the largest in the country and it leads down to the River Ribble. There are good footpaths throughout the park and along the riverbank.

Moor Park: From the M6 junction 31 follow the 'town centre' sign up the hill to the roundabout. Turn right on Blackpool Road for about one mile. Preston North End AFC is on the left. At these traffic lights turn left. Moor Park is on the right and the car park is within a few hundred yards.

# Silloth

Silloth is a small seaside resort. There is ample parking by the harbour and here there are toilets for the disabled. The promenade, which is flat, stretches for 1½ miles. There are more toilets about ¾ mile from the harbour. The main street is virtually parallel to the promenade.

# Tarn Hows

Map ref. 328996. National Trust. Car park and viewpoint.

# Wetherall

Wetherall is an attractive village three miles east of Carlisle, in the Eden Valley. An interesting walk round the village covering the church, green and many places of historical interest.